PELICAN BOOKS

A812

THE ANCIENT GREEKS

M. I. Finley was born in New York City in 1912. He obtained an M.A. in Public Law and a Ph.D. in Ancient History at Columbia University. After working as research assistant in Roman Law at Columbia University in 1933–4, he became editor and translator at the Institute of Social Research (then affiliated to Columbia University) and taught History at the City College of New York. He was Assistant Professor of History at Rutgers University from 1948 to 1952. In 1955 he became a lecturer in the Faculty of Classics at Cambridge and, two years later, was elected a Fellow of Jesus College. He became Reader in Ancient Social and Economic History there in 1964. He has written articles and reviews and is a frequent broadcaster on all aspects of the ancient world. He is the author of *Studies in Land and Credit in Ancient Athens* (1952) and *The World of Odysseus* (1954 – also in Pelicans) and has edited *Slavery in Classical Antiquity* (1960).

M. I. FINLEY

THE ANCIENT GREEKS

PENGUIN BOOKS

IN ASSOCIATION WITH CHATTO & WINDUS

Penguin Books Ltd, Harmondsworth, Middlesex, England
Penguin Books Pty Ltd, Ringwood, Victoria, Australia

—

First published by Chatto & Windus 1963
Published in Pelican Books 1966

—

Copyright © M. I. Finley, 1963

—

Made and printed in Great Britain
by Cox & Wyman Ltd, London,
Fakenham and Reading
Set in Monotype Bembo

TO
PASCAL COVICI

CONTENTS

CONTENTS

MAPS

PLATES

PREFACE

THE first thing that needs to be said in prefacing a book like this is what it is not. I have written neither a narrative nor a reference book. I have tried, instead, to discuss and, where it seemed possible, to explain how Greek civilization developed in its various aspects, its strengths and weaknesses, materially, socially, politically, culturally. The emphases, and the omissions too, reflect my own judgement of what is most interesting and important in Greek history, with one exception which requires special mention. I have not attempted to cope in such a restricted space with technical subjects, whether in poetry, art, philosophy or science. This is a personal analysis, not a summary or least common denominator of the views held by other historians. I hope I have succeeded in distinguishing between a generally accepted fact and an inference, a conclusion, an interpretation of my own; I have tried to suggest in a general way the nature of the evidence; and I have appended a long enough bibliography to provide anyone who wishes with titles to which he may turn either for different interpretations or for detailed studies of special topics and periods. I should also say that Greek civilization after Alexander the Great (the so-called Hellenistic Age) has been treated rather as an epilogue, the Greeks under Roman rule scarcely at all. It was therefore unnecessary to write 'B.C.' after a date except in a few instances where confusion might otherwise arise.

I am deeply grateful to Mr G. S. Kirk and Professor A. Andrewes, who read the manuscript and discussed many points with me; to Professor R. M. Cook, particularly for his help with Chapter 7: to Mr Michael Ayrton, Mr Willard Hutcheon, Professor A. H. M. Jones, Dr W. H. Plommer,

Mr J. G. Pollard and Professor Martin Robertson for their suggestions and criticisms; to Mr Roger Toulmin, who produced the series on the Greeks in Network Three of the B.B.C. early in 1961, for which I wrote the booklet out of which this volume grew; and to my wife, who not only read the final manuscript but lived through all its preliminary stages.

Acknowledgement is made for the pictures in the detailed notes on the plates which appear at the end of the volume.

M.I.F.

27 May 1962

A few minor revisions, particularly in the bibliography, have been made for this edition, and a chronological table has been added.

M.I.F.

13 November 1965

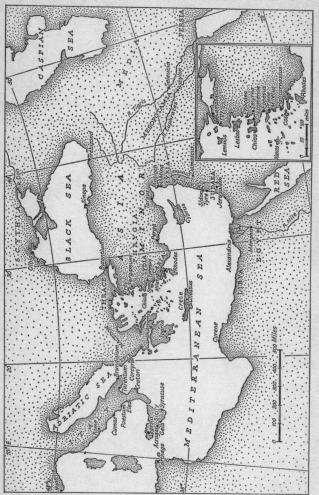

THE GREEK WORLD

CHAPTER I

WHO WERE THE GREEKS?

GREEK-SPEAKING people first migrated southward into the Greek peninsula at the beginning of the second millennium B.C., almost certainly before 1900.* Whatever their cultural level when they entered, they eventually helped fashion the technically advanced Bronze Age civilization of the period 1400–1200 which we call Mycenaean, and which had its main centres in the Peloponnese (the southern part of mainland Greece) at such places as Mycenae, Argos and Pylos. The recent decipherment of their syllabic script – the so-called Linear B (Plate 1a) – has proved that, in the palaces at least, their language was an early form of Greek. That was a startling discovery, but its implications can easily be exaggerated. The southern Balkans had a long Stone Age and Bronze Age history before the Greeks appeared on the scene. What happened on their arrival is unknown apart from the material remains, and these do not show any sudden burst of innovation that can be credited to migrants. On the contrary, more centuries were to go by before the brilliant Mycenaean period was to emerge, and it is impossible to disentangle a 'Greek' contribution to it from the 'pre-Greek', just as it is useless to try to sort out the genetic elements in the biologically mixed stock which now made up the population. Race, language and culture had no simple correlation with each other then, any more than at other times or places in history.

About 1200 Mycenaean civilization came to a fairly abrupt end, and some historians attribute this to a new Greek immigration, that of the Dorians. The following four hundred years were a Dark Age – dark to us, that is to say, because we know

* All dates in this book are B.C. unless otherwise indicated.

(and can know) so little about it. It is tempting also to think of it as 'dark' in the way the Middle Ages used to be known as the Dark Ages: the art of writing disappeared, the centres of power crumbled, there was much petty warfare, tribes and smaller groups migrated within Greece and eastward across the Aegean Sea to Asia Minor, and all in all the material and cultural levels were poverty-stricken by contrast with the Mycenaean civilization. Yet for all that, the story is not just one of decay and decline, for it was in this Dark Age, by a process we can only vaguely glimpse in archaeological finds and in the myths as told by later Greeks, that a major technological revolution occurred – the coming of iron – and that Greek society was born. The old Mycenaean world, despite the Greek language of the palaces, had its closest kinship among their contemporary, highly centralized and bureaucratic states farther east, in northern Syria and Mesopotamia. The new world, the historical Greek world, was (and remained) altogether different, economically, politically and culturally. There were continuities, of course, but they were fragments worked into a new, unrecognizable context. The fundamental technical skills and knowledge in agriculture, pottery-making and metallurgy were retained, and the Greek language survived this social transformation, as it survived all subsequent changes up to the present day.

In their own language the Greeks have never called themselves 'Greeks' (that word comes from the Roman name for them, *Graeci*). In Mycenaean times they were apparently known as Achaeans (judging from contemporary Hittite records), one of several names they still bear in the Homeric poems, the earliest surviving Greek literature. In the course of the Dark Age, or perhaps at its very end, the term 'Hellene' permanently replaced all others, and 'Hellas' became the collective noun for the Greeks taken together. Today Hellas is the name of a country, like France or Italy. In antiquity, however, there was nothing comparable, nothing to which the Hellenes could refer as 'our country'. To them Hellas was essentially an abstraction, like Christendom in the Middle Ages or 'the Arab world' at the present time, for the ancient Greeks were never united politically or territorially.

Eventually Hellas spread over an enormous area, including the Black Sea littoral to the east, the coastal areas of Asia Minor, the Aegean islands, Greece proper, southern Italy and most of Sicily, and continuing west on both shores of the Mediterranean to Cyrene in Libya and to Marseilles and a few Spanish coastal sites. Roughly the area can be visualized as a great ellipse, with the Mediterranean (and the Black Sea as its extension) constituting the long axis; a very flat ellipse, for it was on the edge of the sea, not in the hinterland, that Greek civilization grew and flourished. The roll of the great centres can be called, one by one, without going more than twenty or twenty-five miles inland. Everything behind this thin belt was peripheral, land to be drawn upon for food, metal and slaves, to be raided for booty, to receive Greek manufactured products, but not to be inhabited by Greeks if that could possibly be avoided.

All these far-flung Greeks had a consciousness of belonging to a single culture – 'our being of the same stock and the same speech, our common shrines of the gods and rituals, our similar customs', as Herodotus (VIII 144) phrased it. On the Greek peninsula proper and in the Aegean islands the world they inhabited had become wholly Greek, in fact, except for foreign slaves, foreign transients and occasional oddities like the aboriginal stratum on the island of Samothrace. Elsewhere the Greek communities existed among, and were surrounded by, other peoples. Where the natives were more primitive, such as the Scythians in southern Russia or the Thracians along the northern Aegean or the Sicels and Sicans in Sicily, the Greeks tended to dominate the natives, economically and culturally, and often politically. Where, on the other hand, they were settled in the territory of an advanced and well-organized people, especially in the Persian Empire, they had to accept an overlordship. But even then they succeeded in maintaining a considerable autonomy, in living a wholly Greek way of life and in retaining their Hellenic self-consciousness.

Of course, common civilization never meant absolute identity. There were differences in dialect, in political organization, in cult practices, often in morals and values, sharper in the peripheral areas, but by no means absent in the centre as well. Yet in their own eyes the differences were minor when measured against the common elements of which they were so conscious. Their language, for example, may have varied in dialect, but a Greek from any one place was still understood everywhere else better than an uneducated Neapolitan or Sicilian in Venice today. They all used the same alphabet, adapted about 800 from an earlier Phoenician invention, a system in which the signs represented the simpler sounds of the language rather than syllables, an utterly different script from Linear B and a far superior writing tool (Plate 1). And they lumped everyone else, everyone who did not speak Greek as his native tongue, into the single category of 'barbarian', a man whose speech was unintelligible and sounded like 'bar-bar-bar'. Barbarians were not only unintelligible; they were, many Greeks came to believe, inferior by nature – the highly civilized Egyptians and Persians alongside the Scythians and Thracians.

CHAPTER 2

THE DARK AGE AND THE HOMERIC POEMS

THE Dark Age may have been wholly illiterate and backward in other ways, but it was not devoid of a cultural life. The development of fine pottery with geometric designs (Plate 19) is one example, the Homeric poems another. They leave the historian in a frustrating position, as he tries to reconstruct some four hundred years of history, the formative centuries of historical Greek civilization, out of material remains, two long poems and the later, unreliable traditions and myths of the Greeks.

The Greeks, with few exceptions, understood the *Iliad* and *Odyssey* to be the work of a single poet, Homer. No one was certain when he lived or where (but the island of Chios made the most successful claim). Modern students are divided on the question whether or not both poems were composed by one poet, and on their date. It is now agreed, however, that the author or authors cannot be thought of like later epic poets, such as Virgil or Dante or Milton. Behind the *Iliad* and *Odyssey* lay centuries of oral poetry, composed, recited and transmitted by professional bards without the aid of a single written word. Whereas Virgil could decide as a voluntary act to take the story of Aeneas as the subject of a long epic, and could make it as sophisticated, learned and complicated in language, structure and ideas as he liked, the bard had no such freedom. Partly this was a matter of mere technique, of the severe limits imposed by oral composition; equally it was a matter of social convention. Both the subjects and the manner of composition were fixed. The language was rich, stylized and artificial, admirably suited to the needs of oral composition. The themes were those of an 'heroic' past, believed by the bards and their listeners alike to have been a real past which the poet narrated, rather than invented or created. 'For you sing truly indeed of the fate of the Achaeans . . .,' says Odysseus to the bard Demodocus in the *Odyssey* (VIII 489–91), 'as if you yourself had been present or had heard it from another.'

The return of writing to Greece in the wonderfully flexible shape of the phonetic alphabet then altered the picture radically. It became possible to catch in permanent form and on a large canvas the poetry which had evolved during the centuries of illiteracy. That few poets made the attempt need cause no surprise. What is remarkable is that among them was the man (or men) who produced two of the greatest poems in world literature. We cannot compare the *Iliad* and *Odyssey* with the other heroic poetry written at the end of the Dark Age, for the rest have disappeared along with the bulk of Greek literature in general. The judgement of the ancients, at least, was virtually unanimous in rating the now lost work far below the two surviving poems.

There were a number of heroic themes in Dark Age Greece, but the greatest of them was the massive invasion of Troy and its destruction by a coalition from mainland Greece, and the homecoming of the heroes; all of it embroidered with many minor tales from the lives of the same heroes and from associated activities among the Olympic gods. As the Dark Age went on, the accumulated stock of incidents became very large, and it was in making selections and combinations from them that the poet can be said to have had his freedom of choice. Thus, long as the *Iliad* and *Odyssey* are (nearly 17,000 and 13,000 lines, respectively), they cover only a fraction of the ground, the former concentrating on a few days during the ten-year siege of Troy and ending with the death of Hector (but not going on to the capture of the city), the latter on the ten years' wandering of a single hero, Odysseus, on his way back from Troy to his home in Ithaca.

Archaeologists have shown that Troy was in fact destroyed near the end of the thirteenth century, as some later Greek historians had conjectured, and that many of the places associated with the Homeric heroes were in fact important Mycenaean centres. Something of a genuine, historical Mycenaean kernel therefore remains in the poems, just as bits of the past survive in other examples of heroic poetry, like the medieval French *Song of Roland* or the short Russian lays about Prince Vladimir of Kiev. But not much, and even that is usually distorted. Imperceptibly, and only half-consciously at best, the tales were transformed as they passed from bard to bard and as the period, the events and the society they were 'narrating' receded farther in time and became more and more unintelligible to them. In a sense the poets were trying to do two contradictory things at once: on the one hand they were trying to retain an image of a dead past, and on the other hand they wished to be understood and believed. So, for example, they pictured in words magnificent palaces, which they had never seen and which came to be less and less like the Mycenaean palaces (or any other, for that matter, because their own world had no palaces); or they tried to describe the use of chariots in warfare, an obsolete practice out of which they could make little sense; or they described the bronze weapons of the Mycenaeans but could not prevent iron from creeping in, because now weapons were being made of iron, not of bronze.

Such anachronisms trouble the historian, but neither the bards nor their audiences were historians. For parallels, one might look to Shakespeare's historical plays, or to Renaissance paintings of scenes from Greek history and mythology, or to Bible illustrations in any period. They bristle with inaccuracies, but no one gives that a second thought. The one thing which would not have been tolerated in Greek heroic poetry would have been the intrusion into the narrative of events known to have occurred after the 'heroic' age – the coming of the Dorians, for example. Their absence from the poems was the proof, so to speak, that the poets were re-telling the ancient tales correctly. For the rest – social institutions, attitudes and ideas, codes of behaviour – there could be no control over error for the simple reason that nothing existed in writing. This point cannot be underscored too much. After a century had gone by, it would literally have been impossible to check any claims about the powers of Agamemnon, the size of his army or the details of the battles. The poems, as they were recited, were both the truth itself and the evidence for their own truth.

The society which unfolds in the *Iliad* and *Odyssey* is one of kings and nobles, who possessed much land and many flocks and lived a life of splendour and fighting. The noble household was the centre of activity and power. The king was judge, lawgiver and commander. He was subject to no formal controls, depending on the sanction of his prowess, his wealth and his connexions. A weak king did not long survive the challenge of powerful rivals or outside enemies. He had no 'state' or 'community' which could effectively back him as a matter of law or tradition. Not that this was a jungle world : there were ceremonies, rituals and conventions by which men lived. What was lacking was a sanction strong enough to check or overcome the greatest of all sanctions, that of effective power. When Odysseus was absent, the nobles of Ithaca behaved scandalously towards his family and his possessions while they manoeuvred among themselves to seize his power. A few, like old Mentor, protested, but their words carried no weight, and the poet as much as says, How could they have?

The people of Ithaca remained silent. Indeed, in both poems the population, other than the heroic nobles, are a vague mass whose exact status is altogether unclear. Some, chiefly captive women, are called slaves, but they do not appear to be any worse off than the others. A few craftsmen – the metal-workers, woodworkers, seers and physicians – seem to have a higher status. For the remainder, they do the work in the fields and palaces (but not the trading, which is left to foreigners, Phoenicians in particular, or to the chieftains themselves), they participate in raids and even in the great expedition against Troy, but they do not seem to join in the actual fighting, which is restricted to individual combat among the heavy-armed nobles on both sides. They even meet in assemblies occasionally, but they seem to have neither voice nor vote when it comes to actual decision-making. Once only does a commoner presume to take the floor, in the famous passage in the *Iliad* in which Thersites proposes that the siege of Troy be abandoned. Odysseus promptly beats him over the back and shoulders with a sceptre, putting a quick end to that isolated breach of correct behaviour.

Compared with the real world of the thirteenth century, the Mycenaean world, all this activity is too small in scale and misconceived in character. Modern archaeology and the decipherment of the Linear B tablets between them have made that clear. The Greeks themselves had no knowledge of the existence of a Linear B script and precious little of the archaeology, and what they could not help but see of the ruins – as at Mycenae itself – they regularly misunderstood. Those who lived after the Dark Age, at least, were apparently unaware, for example, that there had once been a Bronze Age in which iron was unknown (Herodotus thought that even the pyramids were constructed with iron tools); or, to come down well into the Dark Age, that geometric pottery was the typical decorated Greek ware and not the work of barbarians. In brief, the later Greeks had no memory whatever of a Mycenaean civilization qualitatively different from their own and divided from it by the Dark Age break. They thought of the rulers of Mycenae and Pylos as their own immediate ancestors and forerunners, speaking socially and spiritually, not just biologically, and they were wrong.

For centuries the Greek interest in their past was only a mythical one. That is to say, they were concerned largely with individual, isolated occurrences of the past (usually involving direct participation of supernatural beings), each of which 'explained' a current practice in cult and ritual or in secular institutions; not with an ordered account of the past arranged systematically in time and place. Eventually some Greeks did develop a genuine sense of, and feeling for, history (not before the fifth century), but then it was too late. The more distant past was gone: there were no records other than the few poems which had finally been written down and the vast, indigestible mass of orally transmitted myths. In consequence, their efforts to reconstruct their own early post-Mycenaean history produced far too simple a picture, apart from specific inaccuracies, lacking the ups-and-downs, the sharp variations in time and place, the massive quality of the changes which characterized the centuries of the Dark Age. We have the advantage of modern archaeology and of the rediscovery of the lost worlds of the Hittites, Assyrians and other ancient peoples of western Asia. We know how complete was the disruption of Mycenaean society (at least at the top); how pivotal Athens was in the retention and dissemination of pottery techniques; that monumental buildings disappeared altogether for perhaps four hundred years; that about the year 1000 small groups of men began to migrate eastward across the Aegean to find toeholds on the Asia Minor coast, small, unstable, agricultural settlements, which in time became the centres of what is sometimes called the Ionian Renaissance. All these things we know, and more, little of which was known to the Greeks themselves after the Dark Age ended.

Yet it would be folly to believe that we can, or ever will be able to, write a *history* of the Dark Age. Archaeology, comparative linguistics and comparative mythology, the testimony of contemporary documents in Syria or Egypt, for all their value, quickly reach absolute limits in the light they can throw. Nothing can make up for the non-existence of contemporary Greek writing, whether narrative or religious or administrative. And so we, like the Greeks, must fall back on the *Iliad* and *Odyssey*. Here again, surprising as it may seem, we know far more than the Greeks, for not only has modern philology made its contribution, but it has been possible both in the last century and in our own to study in living practice the technique of oral, heroic poetry-making, most thoroughly among the South Slavs. What emerges as a reasonably safe conclusion is that, though the narrative is not history, whether Mycenaean or Greek, contrary to the firm belief of the Greeks – and not even the most sceptical of them ever doubted this in essence, much as some rebelled against the Homeric image of the gods and other such aspects of the poems – neither are the *Iliad* and *Odyssey* merely poetic fiction. The society portrayed and the thinking are historical, and that adds an important dimension to the mute material remains.

Historical in what sense? When? That is a very thorny question. Modern opinion on the date of the final composition of the poems (ignoring still later interpolations and revisions which were undoubtedly made) ranges from the late ninth century to the early seventh. Even if one accepts an early date, it is quickly apparent that the world of the poems is not the world in which Homer lived. For one thing, there is too much uniformity: Homer's Achaeans are indistinguishable from each other, and from the Trojans too, for that matter. But ninth-century Thessaly (the home of Achilles) and ninth-century Crete and ninth-century Athens were not all that identical. Dialect differed, social evolution moved in different tempi, political institutions too. More serious still, the jump is too great from the inchoate community of the poems to the

communities which were sufficiently organized, over-popu-
lated and technically advanced to initiate the great Greek
emigration and dispersion that began in the middle of the
eighth century. The gap is equally excessive between the games
organized by Achilles for the funeral of Patroclus, which
occupy much of the twenty-third book of the *Iliad,* and the
Olympic Games. (The later the date one accepts for the
poems, of course, the more acute these difficulties become.)
It looks, therefore, as if the deliberate archaizing of the bards
was partially successful: though they lost virtually all memory
of Mycenaean society, they kept far enough behind the times
to picture with some accuracy the early, rather than the late,
Dark Age – always allowing for anachronistic bits, Mycenaean survivals on the one hand, contemporary notes on the
other.

As any historical novelist (or historian) knows, it is easier to
describe the externals of a past age than to get inside the
people themselves, into their thoughts and feelings. The bards
had an advantage in this respect in the large stock of inherited
'formulas' – standard phrases and lines – which were their
professional tools. Nevertheless, they could not really *think* in
the past. Plato complained in the *Republic* (606E) that there
were Greeks who believed that Homer 'educated Hellas and
. . . that a man ought to regulate the whole of his life by
following this poet'. Few works – and probably none which
are not scriptural – have ever had such a hold on a nation for
so many centuries. Poetic genius alone will not explain the
phenomenon, and surely not mere curiosity about a golden
age. The key lies elsewhere. It was Homer (together with a
very different kind of poet, Hesiod), according to Herodotus
(II 53), who 'first fixed for the Greeks the genealogy of the
gods, gave the gods their titles, divided among them their
honours and functions, and defined their images'. Superficially
this looks a silly remark: Zeus would have been lord on

Olympus even if Homer had never lived. But as is often the case with Herodotus, the subtlety and profundity lie just beneath the surface.

It is sometimes said that the anthropomorphism of the Homeric poems is the most complete, the most extreme, on record; that never before or since have gods been so much like men (apart, of course, from their inability to perish); that this is a terribly naïve view of the divinity. No doubt it is, but it is also something else, something perhaps far more interesting and significant. What a bold step it was, after all, to raise man so high that he could become the image of the gods. And who gave Homer (and Hesiod after him) the authority to intervene in such matters? What they did, both in the action itself and in its substance, implies a human self-consciousness and self-confidence without precedent, and pregnant with limitless possibilities.

A single man, Homer, did not bring about such an intellectual revolution, of course, and there is no evidence, one way or the other, from which to decide whether the bards were even aware that they were participating in one. Nor was the revolution total. The Homeric poems show an unmistakable distaste for snake-gods, fertility rites, orgiastic ceremonies, for the frenzied, Dionysiac or Bacchic side of religion, which was both very old and very tenacious. Such things are scarcely allowed to appear in the poems, yet they remained deeply rooted and widely practised to the end of Greek civilization. Already in the Dark Age, however, some men were in revolt against them, repelled not so much by the crudeness and brutality (there is brutality enough in the *Iliad* and *Odyssey*) as by the intellectual inadequacy and human weakness and inferiority. Then came another 'revolution', the return to Greece of the art of writing. Only a society which can write, can sort out, preserve and transmit its knowledge on paper, is capable of systematic inquiry into its religious beliefs (or any

27

other kind). The first step was a theogony. Here Herodotus is somewhat misleading: Homer shows the beginnings only, and the first proper theogony must be assigned to Hesiod, who belongs to the fully historical world of the Greeks, while Homer stood on the threshold.

In sum, the *Iliad* and *Odyssey* present a number of remarkable paradoxes. Probably no other literature burst into writing for the first time with two poems of such genius; and then they had no worthy successors, since really creative writing turned at once to new forms and new subjects. In most significant respects the two poems look back, insistently so; yet at the same time they point ahead whenever they touch at the heart of man's humanity. In that sense the term 'Dark Age' is most misleading (except to underscore our ignorance about what went on). When some Greeks began to think like this, and in particular when they could write their thoughts down, Greek pre-history was at an end.

PERIODS OF GREEK HISTORY

IT is an accepted convention today to divide the subsequent history of the ancient Greeks into a number of periods, the names of which are merely a form of shorthand (not to be taken literally, or even as particularly meaningful):

ARCHAIC – from 800 or 750 to 500, in round numbers, that is, from the time when the political geography of the Greek peninsula and the Greek coastline of Asia Minor had become reasonably fixed to the era initiated by the Persian Wars.

CLASSICAL – the fifth and fourth centuries, the period of the independent city-states and, viewed in the round, of the greatest cultural achievements in all Greek history.

HELLENISTIC – from the time of Alexander the Great to the Roman conquest of the eastern Mediterranean, centuries in which Greek civilization spread east to such new centres as Alexandria and Antioch, from which a Greek–Macedonian aristocracy ruled large Near-Eastern territories (such as Syria and Egypt) under absolute monarchs.

ROMAN – conventionally dated from the defeat of the forces of Antony and Cleopatra by Augustus at the battle of Actium in 31 B.C., although many Greek communities came under Roman rule piecemeal from the third century B.C. onwards, and despite the fact that the civilization of the eastern Roman Empire remained essentially Hellenistic to the end.

CHAPTER 3

ARCHAIC GREECE

UNTIL almost the close of the archaic period, poetry remains the only written source of information. But now the poetry was fundamentally contemporary and personal, apart from a few works in the old heroic style narrating the traditional tales and interweaving them with the familiar accounts of the doings of the gods. The poetry which was alive and fresh moved quickly and decisively away from that tradition. Even when its themes were mythical, its concern was in the final analysis with the present: so Hesiod's *Theogony* and even the so-called (and miscalled) 'Homeric Hymns' tried to introduce some measure of order into the chaotic mass of myths – in itself an impressively new kind of activity and a new conception – and thereby they linked the myths directly and systematically to the rituals and ceremonials which ruled their own lives. This was still neither philosophy nor theology, but it was closer to both than to the spasmodic, far more rudimentary thinking reflected even in the *Iliad* and *Odyssey*.

Hesiod is like Homer in one respect: he is also identified as the author of two long poems in epic form and metre (and of a number of others now known only from surviving fragments), and it is by no means certain that the attribution to a single poet is correct. But there, and in a certain similarity in language, the parallel stops completely. The Hesiod who wrote the *Works and Days* (and the majority view is that he also wrote the *Theogony*) is someone we know intimately as a person – because he tells us much about himself. His father had come from Asia Minor as a refugee to Boeotia. There he farmed, and when he died his estate was the subject of a bitter dispute between his two sons. Hesiod was both bard and farmer, and the main theme of the *Works and Days,* written, it seems, late in the eighth century or early in the seventh, is the life of the farmer, his toil and routines, his slaves and hired hands and oxen, his dislike of the nobles and their injustice on the one hand and of the sea and its small merchant craft on the other, his minute technical knowledge of farming and of the many ritual acts and taboos which went with it, and his perpetual fear of disaster and poverty. Nothing could be more unlike the Homeric poems in subject or outlook.

THE GREEK MAINLAND

31

Similarly with lyric poetry – a radically new kind of literature – as early as Archilochus, a freebooter and mercenary from Paros who may be dated to the middle of the seventh century. He wrote about himself, his friends and enemies in a way which was not only personal but altogether unheroic.

> I hate the lanky officer, stiff-standing, legs apart,
>   Whose cut of hair and whisker is his principal renown;
>   I prefer the little fellow with his bigness in his heart,
>   And let his legs be bandy, if they never let him down.*

There was no more looking back to a dimly perceived great past, but an overriding concern with the present.

The three centuries which make up the archaic period were marked by very considerable development and differentiation, and generalizations must be made with caution and much qualification. This is immediately clear if, for example, one compares the poems of Archilochus with those of Alcaeus half a century later, or both with the latter's contemporaries Sappho and Solon. The differences are not merely a matter of personal temperament and interests but also of political and social distinctions in time and place. The historian of the Greeks must reckon henceforth with a very uneven development, despite all the common elements.

In the more advanced areas of the Greek and Asia Minor mainlands and on the Aegean islands there were now a large number of established communities in the proper sense of that term; something which was missing from the world of the Homeric poems on the one hand, but which was yet rudimentary and incomplete when measured against the fully developed city-state that lay ahead. It is symbolic that when large-scale building returned it was the temple which emerged, and then city walls, not the palace. These archaic communities were invariably small, numbering their inhabitants in

* Translated by Denys Page, *The Listener*, 15 January 1959, pp. 109-10.

the thousands, and independent (unless subjected by conquest). In part, geography explains this fragmentation Much
of the terrain is a chequer-board of mountains and small plains
or valleys, tending to isolate each pocket of habitation from
the other. Land communication from one pocket to another
was rarely easy and sometimes nearly impossible, especially in
the face of resistance. Understandably, therefore, in the period
which followed the Mycenaean break-up, when there was
much movement of invaders and refugees, the small isolated
settlement became the rule. But the geography cannot explain
the later history, why Athens, for example, succeeded in sup-
pressing this tendency in the relatively large district of Attica
and brought the whole area into one city-state, whereas
Thebes failed in repeated attempts to accomplish the same
result in the not much larger neighbouring district of Boeotia,
so that twelve separate city-states survived there; why a little
island like Amorgos had three distinct city-states right through
the classical era; or why, above all, the Greeks carried their
small community to regions like Sicily and southern Italy,
where both geography and self-preservation should have
argued for greater political unity. The tenacity of the small
independent community can be explained only as a habit
which amounted to a deep and ineradicable conviction about
how living together ought to be arranged. By the time the
Greek dispersion east and west was completed, the total of
these more or less independent communities was perhaps
fifteen hundred.

In no respect was the unevenness of development more
marked than in the matter of urbanization. From a purely
residential viewpoint, the Mediterranean pattern seems always
to have been one of clustering in villages or about citadels or
palace-complexes, in preference to the scattered farm-home-
stead. From the community viewpoint, there had to be one
centre where the main civic and religious buildings could be

concentrated and where the citizens could be assembled when necessary (the Agora in its original sense, long before that word came also to mean 'market-place'). Usually there was also an Acropolis, a high point to serve as a citadel for defence. Then the variations begin. In Old Smyrna, for example, one of the first of the settlements in Asia Minor, everyone seems to have lived huddled behind the city walls – an obvious necessity for a small weak group who crossed the Aegean round about the year 1000 to establish a new life in an alien and no doubt hostile world. But the Spartans always resided in villages (or in barracks, which are irrelevant to this discussion), and then there was a third 'type' in which the population was divided between an urban sector and the countryside. These differences were, of course, not merely whimsical, but reactions to different internal and external situations, of wealth and strength and economic development. Sharpest of all were the economic differences, as between Corinth and Miletus, say, on the one hand, and Sparta or the communities of Elis or Arcadia on the other. If one calls the centres in the latter urban, that is essentially a courtesy title, for the whole population lived off agriculture and tribute (whether from fighting or from the income of a shrine) and nothing else, whereas cities like the former included men whose livelihood came from trade and manufacture, and who were therefore economically separated from the land. They were a minor fraction of the population, but their very existence introduced a new dimension into the quality of the community and its structure.

Whatever the pattern in any given instance, it remained true of all of them that town and country were conceived as a single unit, not – as was common in medieval cities – as two antagonistic parties. The whole was bound together not merely by economics or by force, but also psychologically, by a feeling among the members of the community of a unity fostered by common cult and tradition (both mythical and historical). Thus an ancient Greek could only express the idea of Athens as a political unit by saying 'the Athenians'; the single word 'Athens' never meant anything but a spot on the map, a purely and narrowly geographical notion. One travelled to Athens; one made war against the Athenians. The Greeks, in sum, thought of themselves not only as Greeks (Hellenes) as against the barbarians but also and more immediately as members of groups and sub-groups within Hellas. A citizen of Thebes was a Theban and a Boeotian as well as a Greek, and each term had its own emotional meaning backed by special myths. And there were still other groupings, such as 'tribes' inside the community or larger abstractions outside it (like Dorians or Ionians), to make up a complicated and sometimes even contradictory structure of memberships and loyalties.

Politically, however, the individual community alone had a clear and unequivocal existence. The kings and chieftains had disappeared by the end of the Dark Age – so quietly that they left no memory, no tradition, of their overthrow (unlike the parallel stage in Rome, for example). Even the occasional survivals, like the dual monarchs of Sparta, were hereditary generals and priests, not rulers. Power had passed to small groups of aristocratic families who monopolized much, if not all, of the land and ruled partly through formal institutions, councils and magistracies; partly by marital and kinship connexions as an Establishment; partly by the intangible authority which came from their ancestry, for they could all produce genealogies taking them back to famous 'heroes' (and from there, often enough, to one of the gods).

Between the nobility and the rest of the population there were tensions and, increasingly, open conflict, to which a number of developments contributed. One was population growth. No figures are available (not even good guesses)

but the archaeological evidence is clear on this. Neither mainland Greece nor the Aegean islands could support a sizeable
agrarian population, and the surplus could not be absorbed in
other pursuits. Further, the system of land tenure and the laws
of debt were such that not only did the nobility hold the most
land and the best land, but many 'free' men were compelled
to serve as the necessary (but involuntary) labour force for
the larger estates. As Aristotle wrote in his *Constitution of
Athens* (II), 'there was civil strife between the nobles and the
people for a long time' because 'the poor, with their wives
and children, were enslaved to the rich' and 'had no political
rights'.

Yet another factor was military. By a process we cannot
trace but for which there is evidence in vase-paintings soon
after 700, the Homeric warrior was replaced by the hoplite,
the heavy-armed infantryman who fought in massed formation. Hoplites were men of some means, since they had to
provide their own armour and equipment, but many came
from the middle strata who were outside the closed aristocracy, and who, therefore, were a potential counterweight in
the political struggles.

Colonization

For a considerable period a safety-valve was provided by the
mis-named 'colonization' movement, which took off surplus
(and disaffected) sections of the population to new regions.
Ancient accounts of this movement are remarkably unhelpful,
with their mythical elements and their emphasis on a few
individuals and their quarrels rather than on the broader social
aspects. One reasonably sober example, the story of the foundation of Syracuse preserved by the geographer Strabo, who
lived 700 years after the event, reads like this (VI 2, 4):

Archias, sailing from Corinth, founded Syracuse about the same time that Naxos and Megara [also in Sicily] were established. They say that when Myscellus and Archias went to Delphi to consult the oracle, the god asked whether they preferred wealth or health. Archias chose wealth and Myscellus health, and the oracle then assigned Syracuse to the former to found and Croton [in southern Italy] to the latter. . . . On his way to Sicily, Archias left a part of the expedition . . . to settle the island now called Corcyra [modern Corfu]. . . . The latter expelled the Liburni who occupied it and established a settlement. Archias, continuing on his journey, met with some Dorians . . . who had separated from the settlers of Megara; he took them with him and together they founded Syracuse.

This tells us very little. It is true that the colonizing expeditions were led by 'founders', that the oracle at Delphi was often consulted, that the migrants were prepared to fight, subjugate or expel natives, that colonizing groups from two or more cities frequently joined efforts. But though the Dark Age drift to Asia Minor may have been haphazard and chancy, a flight rather than an orderly emigration, the new movement was certainly not. Archias' expedition to Syracuse would not have been possible unless Corinth had attained sufficient size, wealth and political organization to arrange it – to provide the ships, arms and equipment, the leaders, land surveyors and other skilled men who would be needed on arrival – and unless Corinth were driven to it as well. The element of compulsion is basic: nothing else would have generated so continuous a movement on so vast a scale, relatively speaking, for so long a time; nothing else would have supplied the migrants or forced their communities to let them go and, when necessary, make them go.

Loosely, one may speak of two waves of colonization. The first, beginning about 750, went west: to the islands and coast of the Ionian Sea, to Sicily and southern Italy, and finally (late in the seventh century) to Libya and southern France.

37

The second, after a preliminary movement to the Thracian coast and Sea of Marmora, entered the Black Sea soon after 650 and eventually encircled most of it with Greek communities. The second wave was dominated by two cities, Megara in Greece proper and Miletus in Asia Minor, whereas western colonization was widely shared. Corinth and the two cities of Chalcis and Eretria in the island of Euboea started the process; then came Megara, Troezen, the districts of Achaea and Locris, Phocaea in Asia Minor, Rhodes, cities in Crete, some of the colonies themselves, such as Gela, and even Sparta (according to a badly confused tradition about the foundation of Tarentum) and the tiny island of Thera (modern Santorini). This list is incomplete, but it is sufficient to reveal that there was little correlation between type of community and colonizing activity; that the only thing these varied 'mother-cities' had in common was a condition of crisis.

The Greek word we conventionally translate as 'colony' is *apoikia,* which connotes 'emigration'. The point to be stressed is that each was, from the outset and by intention, an independent Greek community, not a colony as that word is customarily understood. And since the movement was an answer to demographic and agrarian difficulties, the new communities were themselves agricultural settlements, not trading-posts (in contrast to the Phoenician colonies in the west). Hence, numerous as were the 'colonies' in southern Italy, there was none at the best harbour on the east coast, the site of Roman Brundisium (modern Brindisi). Hence, too, the aristocracy of the greatest of the new communities, Syracuse, were called *Gamoroi,* which means 'those who shared the land, landowners'.

There were a few genuine trading-posts, it should be said, such as the recently discovered one at Al Mina at the mouth of the Orontes in northern Syria, established early in the eighth century, probably before even the first of the 'colonies'; or the later posts called Emporium (which means in Greek more or less what it means in English) in Spain and at the mouth of the Don on the Black Sea. Notably their number was very few, and normally they did not grow into genuine communities. This contrast with the 'colonies' helps place archaic Greek commercial development in its proper proportions. 'If desire for uncomfortable sea-faring seize you,' Hesiod advised his brother (*Works and Days* 618–49); 'if ever you turn your misguided heart to trading,' I, who 'have no skill in sea-faring nor in ships,' can tell you this: 'Admire a small ship, but put your freight in a large one; for the greater the lading, the greater will be your piled gain, if only the winds will keep back their harmful gales.'* Hesiod's dislike cannot conceal the fact that already in his time maritime trade was profitable, though risky. The cargoes were primarily agricultural – stimulated by the increasing emphasis, especially among large landowners, on olive and wine production, for which the soil was so well suited; the return cargoes were metals, regional products like hides and furs, and from the sixth century on, slaves in increasing numbers. But the scale and the total volume were small; Greek civilization remained rooted in the soil, and this was true even of the most highly urbanized communities like Athens or Corinth or Miletus.

Above all, the relation between 'colony' and 'mother-city' was neither commercially based nor imperialistic in other ways. To be sure, when Corinth was the chief exporter of fine painted pottery, she sold them to her colonies, and through them to Etruscans and other non-Greek peoples who acquired a taste for them. But she sold them equally to other colonies, and when Athens took that trade away from her about the middle of the sixth century there was no visible change in 'colonial relations'. Nor was there a visible decline in Corinthian wealth or prosperity; nor did Athens' new commercial dominance (in this one field at least) require her to seek her

* Translated by H. G. Evelyn-White in the Loeb Classical Library.

own colonial outlets. Indeed, it has been well said that it was precisely because the colonies were independent from the start, both politically and economically, that on the whole they maintained close friendly relations with their respective mother-cities for many years – based on tradition and cult, free from the irritations and conflicts often aroused elsewhere by commercial disputes and rivalries.

Tyrants and Lawgivers

The hiving-off process failed to eliminate the difficulties at home. 'Redistribute the land and cancel debts' was the cry heard all over, within a few generations even in some of the new settlements. Nor was the aristocracy always united: factious and ambitious individuals often brought about struggles for power within their ranks, exacerbating the troubles. Out of this civil strife, and aided by the new military developments, there arose the specifically Greek institution of the tyrant. Originally a neutral word, 'tyrant' signified that a man seized and held power without legitimate constitutional authority (unlike a king); it implied no judgement about his quality as a person or ruler. Individual tyrants in fact varied very much: some, like Peisistratus in Athens, reigned benevolently and well, put an end to civil war, helped solve the economic problems and advanced their cities in many ways. But uncontrolled military power was inherently an evil; if not in the first generation, then in the second or third the tyrants usually became what the word now means.

Some cities escaped tyranny altogether, the most famous instance being Sparta. She was in a unique position: having conquered and permanently subjugated the people of Laconia very early (no doubt in the Dark Age), she then subjected Messenia to the same treatment. Possessing very extensive and fertile lands and a large servile labour force (called 'helots') in consequence, the Spartans created a military-political organization without parallel, and they were long immune from both the economic and the political troubles characteristic of most archaic Greek states. Traditionally this system was the work of a single 'lawgiver', Lycurgus. Modern scholars are not even agreed on whether such a man existed at all, let alone on his date or what he actually did. Much of the tradition about him cannot be right, and it seems corrupted beyond rescue. It is a fact, but one which proves nothing one way or the other about Lycurgus, that the lawgiver was not a rare figure in archaic Greece – one thinks especially of Solon in early sixth-century Athens, but also of lesser names like Zaleucus and Charondas among the western Greeks. The laws, constitutional, civil, sacral and criminal, had to be fixed and codified if the community were to emerge from its embryonic state, in which a handful of families controlled all the resources and all the sanctions ('bribe-devouring judges', Hesiod called them). There were no precedents to fall back on either, giving room for free invention as men tried to think up ways by which a state could be administered, power distributed, laws passed and enforced.

The lack of precedent can hardly be over-stated; in whatever field the archaic Greeks made new moves, no matter what the motive, they rarely had models to imitate or improve upon. This situation of compulsory originality, so to speak, is visible in many aspects of their life: in the individualism of their lyric poetry; in their new public architecture; in Hesiod – both the Hesiod of the *Theogony* and the Hesiod of the *Works and Days* – with his rare presumption which led him (or them) to tamper with the traditions about his gods and to judge the behaviour of his earthly rulers; in the speculative philosophers, who began to inquire, again on their own authority and supported only by their own mental faculties, into the nature of the universe; and in politics, where the originality is more easily overlooked. In the instance of the lawgiver about whom we know most, Solon, it was present in the very action which brought him to that position. The Athenian class struggle had reached an impasse and in 594 Solon was *chosen*, by agreement, charged with the task of reforming the state. That is the point; he was chosen by the Athenians themselves, on their own initiative and their own authority, because he was respected for his wisdom and righteousness. He was not 'called' and he had no vocation. Nor did he seize power as a tyrant.

Solon, like the other lawgivers, agreed that justice came from the gods, of course, but he made no claim to a divine mission or even, in any significant sense, to divine guidance. 'I gave the common people such privilege as is sufficient,' he wrote in one of his poems. As to those in power, 'I saw to it that they should suffer no injustice. I stood covering both parties with a strong shield, permitting neither to triumph unjustly.' Superficially, there may seem to be a resemblance with Hammurabi's preamble to his famous code, a thousand years earlier; the Babylonian monarch also said that his aim was 'to make justice to appear in the land, to destroy the evil and the wicked that the strong might not oppress the weak'. But the distinctions are far more important and consequential. In the first place, there is the secular quality of the Greek codification, whereas Hammurabi acted in the name of the gods. And then there is the decisive fact that the Eastern king legislated for subjects, the Greek lawgiver laid down rules by which the community should govern itself. Having completed his work, in fact, Solon left Athens for ten years so that the community could test his programme without prejudice; his own great prestige, he feared, might otherwise weight the balance of judgement unfairly.

In one sense Solon failed. He did not solve the economic

difficulties lying behind the civil strife and after a generation tyranny, which he sought to stave off, came to Athens. Yet Solon remained in the memory of later Athenians, regardless of party, as the man who finally set them on the path to greatness. When Aristotle summed up Solon's achievements in his brief account of the Athenian constitution he chose the following three as the most crucial: abolition of enslavement for debt, creation of the right of a third party to seek justice in court on behalf of an aggrieved person and the introduction of appeals to a popular tribunal. All three had one thing in common: they were steps designed to advance the community idea (and reality) by protecting the weaker majority from the excessive and, so to speak, extra-legal power of the nobility. Or, stated differently, they stopped up loopholes in the rule of law, an idea which was coming to be the Greek definition of civilized political organization; more than that, they were steps towards equality before the law, which Athenians in the classical period considered the central feature of democracy.

The role of the great Athenian tyrant Peisistratus in this development was paradoxical. By his very existence as tyrant he breached the idea of rule by law. On the other hand, later writers generally praised him, much as they condemned tyranny as an institution, because, in actual practice, 'he wished to govern according to the laws without giving himself any prerogatives' (Aristotle, *Const. of Athens* XVI 8). This cannot be accepted as literally true, but it is not simply untrue either. Using different techniques, and no doubt acting from altogether different motives, Peisistratus nevertheless carried Athens a very long way along the road Solon had sketched out. Himself a member of the nobility (he traced his ancestry to Nestor, the Homeric king of Pylos), he refused to play their game against the peasantry and the dispossessed. Indeed, being a tyrant, he could accomplish what Solon could not, and it was in his reign that the peasantry finally obtained a reasonably

43

secure and independent position on the land, with financial assistance when required, that the civil strife was abated and that the political monopoly of the aristocratic families was broken once and for all. Nobles continued to hold the leading civil and military offices – as they did well into the next century under the democracy, too – but the circumstances and the psychology were radically altered. They were now, increasingly, servants of the state, instruments of the law, and not arbitrary wielders of power; just as the common people were now genuinely free men, no longer threatened with debt bondage or with wholly partisan justice. The two factions were far from equals, but at least the differences between them had been reduced to a workable scale and proportion.

Peisistratus was in power from 545 (after one or two brief spells before that) until his death in 527, succeeded by his elder son Hippias, who was expelled in 510. For thirty years this was a peaceful rule, a time when Athens advanced rapidly in power and wealth, and when there were many new visible signs of this growth and of the spirit of community – one might almost say 'nationalism' – which accompanied it: in public works and in great religious festivals particularly. But in 514 Hippias' younger brother Hipparchus was assassinated by an embittered rival in a love affair with a young boy, and the tyranny quickly turned into a cruel despotism and was overthrown. In one way or another this story was repeated in many Greek cities from the latter part of the seventh century to the end of the sixth. Tyranny never sat so securely that it was not easily brutalized, because of some incident, or for no reason at all, and then the tyrant was usually thrown out. The institution therefore tended to be ephemeral (with the notable exception of Sicily). But its historical significance cannot be judged by its duration, for tyranny was often the decisive feature in the transitional stage from the personal, familial rule of the nobility to the classical city-state.

None of this was a matter of intention or design. No tyrant, not even Peisistratus, saw himself as the bearer of the historic destiny of the Greeks, as the forerunner of Athenian democracy or of anything else (nor did Solon, for that matter). They wanted power and success, and if they were intelligent and disciplined, like Peisistratus, they gained it by advancing their communities. Solon may have thought that he 'stood covering both parties with a strong shield', but it was Peisistratus and Hippias who in fact had the necessary strength. Solon was followed by a renewal of the old civil war; Hippias, after a very short struggle lasting less than two years, by a wholly new, democratic state.

That was in Athens. The development in other cities took other lines: the unevenness of development already noticed was to remain a feature of Greek history at all times. The most backward regions, like Aetolia or Acarnania, were scarcely affected by this whole trend, but they, by and large, counted for little anyway (except as so much manpower available for war and piracy). Sparta went its own way, the Sicilian cities theirs, each because of special circumstances – the presence of a subjugated servile population or the constant threat of an external power like Carthage. Sometimes, as in Corinth, the nobility remained strong enough to impose an oligarchy for a very long time. And in much of Greece the struggle between 'the few' and 'the many' (in their own phrasing) was never permanently stilled. Nevertheless, the generalization can be made that by the end of the archaic period, and in particular wherever there had been a phase of tyranny, the form of government, whether more democratic or more oligarchical, was on a different level of political sophistication from anything that had come before. This was the period in which some among the Greeks achieved a workable compromise between the competing and, historically speaking, often irreconcilable demands of social obligation and personal freedom;

in which, indeed, they may be said to have discovered the idea of freedom, as distinct from the personal, fundamentally asocial power of the Homeric chieftains, the privilege of the aristocratic families or the anarchy of the freebooters. The imperfections and the mistakes, both on the way and in the final product, cannot diminish the achievement.

The new freedom and the new kind of community rested on economic independence, for most men in agriculture, for the rest in trade and manufacture or in the arts. Wherever debt bondage and other ancient kinds of dependent labour were abolished it was necessary to turn to a new source, the chattel slave, whether captive Greek or, with increasing frequency, the barbarian. The sixth century was the turning-point on this score also. The first indication we have of demo-cratic institutions is in a fragmentary text from the island of Chios, dated between 575 and 550. It was Chios, too, which according to a confused but very insistent Greek tradition first began to buy slaves from the barbarians. This can scarcely be very accurate history, but the symbolism is just right. After all, it was Athens which was to become the largest slave-holding state in classical Greece. The final paradox, therefore, of archaic Greek history is this march hand in hand of freedom and slavery.

The Community, Religion and Pan-Hellenism

Then, as today, the visible external sign of all this growth in prosperity and political maturity was the temple. The origins of the Greek temple are lost in the Dark Age; neither wood nor sun-dried brick leaves traces as a rule, and no temple in stone can be dated with certainty before the seventh century. Then they began to appear at an accelerated tempo, as tech-nical skills ripened and, even more important, as the power grew to mobilize the necessary resources in men and materials, no light task for small communities with primarily agrarian populations equipped with poor transport and only simple tools. The impetus must have been a powerful one, and it is not surprising that the great tyrants, in particular, were great temple-builders. One is tempted to draw a parallel with medieval monarchs and their cathedrals, but that is somewhat misleading, for the temple was a house for a god, not a place of worship. The rituals by which one gave thanks to the Olympic gods or pleaded with them or appeased them required no temple but an altar; and altars existed everywhere, in the homes and fields, in the places of assembly, outside the temples – everywhere, that is, but not inside a temple. One also celebrated one's gods on stated occasions by processions, games and festivals. Then the god was brought from the temple, or there might be a statue of him in the stadium or theatre; but again, nothing happened within the temple itself.

In a sense the temple was a monument to the community, a conspicuous demonstration of its greatness, strength and, above all, self-consciousness. Not even tyrants built palaces or splendid tombs in self-glorification; Peisistratus lived on the Acropolis for a time, but his 'memorial' there was the temple of Athena Parthenos (destroyed by the Persians in 480 and subsequently replaced by the Parthenon). This, like his Fountain-House, reveals how far the Greek community had advanced as a living force, so that even a tyrant bowed to it, and how different their politics had become from Mycenaean and Near-Eastern states, on the one hand, and in another way, from their own 'heroic age'. Homer's heroes lived on in the tales of their feats of prowess, now men immortalized themselves in public buildings – collectively rather than in-dividually.

This is not to say that there was no religious feeling in-volved. The difficulty lies in trying to sort out the strands in any given action or behaviour-pattern. The Greek word for 'priest' is *hiereus*, and the first and most striking thing about the word is that it was usually applied to what we should call laymen, to officials of the state whose function it was to carry out the rituals and who lacked any of the peculiar training, inspiration or sanctity one associates with priests in modern religions (or in many ancient ones). They were officials in exactly the same sense as generals or treasurers or market commissioners, with the same backgrounds of family, wealth, experience, with the same tenure and rotation of office, as the others. The rules under which they functioned were also laid down by the state, through its regular organs. Much of Solon's codification, for example, was devoted not to constitutional or economic measures but to the minute details of sacrifice. Even when, as with the cult of Demeter at Eleusis in the south-western corner of Attica, administration was the prerogative of two ancient aristocratic families, the Eumolpids and the Kerykes, they were still laymen and not a hereditary priestly caste like the Magi or Brahmins.

All this can be traced in a direct line from what is found in the earliest Greek records. In the Homeric poems it was Nestor or Agamemnon who sacrificed as rulers or as heads of households. Now the state had replaced the princes in power, and therefore it took over their priestly duties as well. A 'memory' of the past sometimes survived, as in the case of the two kings of Sparta, who were the chief religious officials of the state; or in Athens, where the highest cult official was one of the nine annually elected archons but was referred to simply as 'the king'. Furthermore, just as the state subsumed a variety of smaller groupings which retained various public functions, so religion was practised on those levels too. There were shrines within each household, there were shrines of the parishes (demes), and there were countless private societies, each organized around the cult of a particular god or of a divine hero like Heracles or Achilles. And on the lower levels the ritual was also the duty of laymen.

Among the factors which made such a pattern possible was the persistent anthropomorphism of Greek religion, with its stress on this world rather than on an after-life. In so far as the gods were like men, relations between men and the gods had a familiar quality, that of a *quid pro quo*. And just as human relations were most satisfactory when they were governed by acknowledged rules and ceremonials, so were relations with the immortals. The main difference between the two sets of rules was that the religious ones were more conventional, less rational, in the sense that unless one were actually told the reason in each particular instance, one could not work out the explanation for oneself by ordinary logic. Why, for example, was the cult of Demeter centred in Eleusis? Anyone who asked that question would have been told a story (the best version is the beautiful 'hymn' to Demeter, one of the so-called 'Homeric Hymns') : Demeter wandered over the earth in search of her daughter Persephone, who had been kidnapped by Hades, she arrived in Eleusis in disguise and so forth. There was a story – a myth – for every sacred site and every sacral act. The myth 'explained' the ritual. It took the place of theology, so to speak, and it was accessible to everyone.

The end-product was not a tidy one. The longest of the Homeric Hymns is about Apollo and it has two distinct parts which are incoherent, if not inconsistent, one linking the god with Delphi, the other with Delos, his two most important shrines. Similar inconsistencies can be multiplied a thousand-fold, as anyone can see by looking into any modern handbook of Greek mythology. A succession of lay practitioners in hundreds of autonomous communities scattered over a very large area, working often with orally transmitted myths, would have introduced confusion enough in the course of three or four centuries without the interference of partisan interests.

But such interests were far from rare. Eleusis, for example, had been an independent community; then she was incorporated into Athens, not later than the end of the seventh century, whereupon Athens successfully appropriated both the cult and the prestige among Greeks generally that went with it. All Greeks recognized and honoured the whole pantheon, but each city had its particular patron deity and its special affinities with individual gods and demi-gods, just as each god had his or her favourite shrines. Each city therefore worshipped Zeus or Apollo or Demeter as its own private affair. There was no 'mother church', no national priesthood, no central authority on ritual, let alone doctrine.

Nor does the complexity stop there. Religion was the business of the state or community, but the latter never held a monopoly. The state, whatever its form, could not so control the gods that it could prevent them from communicating directly with individuals, rather than 'through channels'. In one striking form they communicate with everyone: everyone dreams. Everyone also observes birds in flight, streaks of lightning, the darting of flames and other 'natural' phenomena. But few could interpret them correctly: the god himself chose those who would really hear his message and understand it. The seer or soothsayer tended to be a private individual (from the Homeric poems to the end of Greek civilization), whose skill was esoteric and mystical, whose power and success rested not in any office he held but on the purely pragmatic test of whether or not he found a following, men or even whole communities who accepted his secret knowledge and acted on it.

Sometimes the two aspects of religion were combined. The official priests of Delphi were lay administrators, according to the normal pattern, but the paramount standing of that particular sanctuary came from its oracle, from Apollo himself, who answered questions by speaking through a woman called the Pythia or Pythoness, and she was, in the strict sense, a medium. Other cults found different combinations. The one at Eleusis was a mystery cult (that is the technical Greek term for it), involving not only the usual public procession administered by public officials but also a purification rite and a final, secret initiation.

Polytheism tends always to be pragmatic. When a shrine like Delphi proves to be authentic its appeal quickly transcends its own immediate geographical and political sphere. According to tradition, Delphi was regularly consulted about the foundation of colonies, and that would put its pan-Hellenic character back to the middle of the eighth century. Much of the tradition, however, looks too obviously like later invention, and there is also considerable archaeological evidence to suggest that Delphi was a rather localized shrine in the eighth century which then acquired swift momentum, to become truly pan-Hellenic in the following century. Once it achieved that status, some (though by no means all) of the new settlements which had had no Delphic sanction acquired it retrospectively – providing one more example of the legendary element which is so strong in the 'traditions' about the early archaic period. On the other hand, another type of pan-Hellenic shrine surely goes back to the early eighth century; the traditional date of the founding of the Olympic Games in honour of Zeus is 776, and there is reason to believe that this is an exact date, the first fixed date in Greek history.

Delphi and Olympia each became paramount, the one as oracle, the other as a festival centre (every four years). But they were not unique. Greeks travelled great distances to consult the oracle at Dodona in Epirus, for example, or at Claros in Asia Minor, as they came from all over to participate in or merely to watch the various competitions in the Pythian Games at Delphi or the Isthmian and Nemean Games, both near Corinth. Many others can be named in addition, but on the whole they lacked the pan-Hellenic flavour shared by only a few. It was in this sphere, and in the poetry, drama, architecture, sculpture and athletics associated with it, that one can speak of a genuine pan-Hellenism already in existence in the archaic period. And in this sphere alone – not even religion was able otherwise to break down the particularism of the Greeks and the remarkable indifference and even hostility to each other which were its concomitant. Greeks rarely showed any reluctance to enslave fellow-Greeks or to go to war with each other. Nor was their religion a religion of peace: the Olympian gods were a quarrelsome lot who had come to power through a singularly brutal struggle with their predecessors, the Titans, and they included in their number Ares, the god of war, whereas Eirene was only one of a host of subordinate female deities attendant on the great gods. Apollo was regularly consulted at Delphi before a war was undertaken, but it is not on record that he ever recommended peace as a good in itself, though he sometimes advised against a particular venture simply on its merits.

It would be naïve to believe that a state which was determined to invade a neighbour would easily have been dissuaded by the 'crooked and ambiguous utterances' of the oracle, as Aeschylus characterized them. War and peace were normally determined by more mundane considerations. The tyrants, in fact, were the most powerful factor for peace known in the archaic age. Because their position at home was never very stable, they were afraid of foreign war and they were generally successful in avoiding it, bulwarking themselves behind a network of alliances with each other, usually cemented by dynastic marriages. And yet, it would also be wrong to take the purely cynical view that the Delphic priests were without political intelligence or influence. No society plays a meaningless game like that for three or four centuries, and pays for it heavily to boot (as the great accumulation of treasure at Delphi testifies so eloquently). Whether we are able to penetrate their psychology or not, the Greeks with hardly an exception took Delphi seriously. But they also took it in their stride. The untidiness and many contradictions in their myths and rituals fall in the same category. They trouble the modern student, and they troubled a few ancient students as well, such men as Xenophanes or Herodotus or Plato, each in his own way. Few *studied* the myths, however; the rest performed the rites and that was sufficient.

CHAPTER 4

THE CLASSICAL CITY-STATE

THE Greek word *polis* (from which we derive words like 'political') in its classical sense meant 'a self-governing state'. However, because the *polis* was always small in area and population, the long-standing convention has been to render it 'city-state', a practice not without misleading implications. The biggest of them, Athens, was a very small state indeed by modern standards – about 1,000 square miles, roughly equivalent to Dorset or Derbyshire or the duchy of Luxemburg – but to call it a *city*-state gives a doubly wrong stress; it overlooks the rural population, who were the majority of the citizen body, and it suggests that the city ruled the country, which is inaccurate. And Athens, in the extent and quality of its urbanization, stood at one end of the Greek spectrum together with a relatively small number of other states. At the other end were many which were not cities at all, though they all possessed civic centres. When Sparta, for example, in 385 defeated Mantinea, then the leading *polis* in Arcadia, her terms were that the 'city' be razed and the people return to the villages in which they had once lived. It is clear from Xenophon's account that the hardship caused was only political and psychological: the inhabitants of the 'city' of Mantinea were the owners of landed estates, who preferred to live together in the centre, away from their farms, in a style visible as far back as the Homeric poems and which had nothing else to do with city-life.

How small the scale really was can best be indicated by a few numbers, all of them estimates, since no exact figures are available. When the Athenian population was at its peak, at the outbreak of the Peloponnesian War in 431, the total, including men, women and children, free and slave, was about 250,000 or perhaps 275,000. With the possible exception of Syracuse, which is not properly comparable for various reasons, no other Greek *polis* ever approached that figure until the Roman period with its altogether changed conditions. Corinth may have counted 90,000, Thebes, Argos, Corcyra and Acragas 40,000–60,000 each, and the rest tailed off, many to 5,000 and even fewer. Space was equally compact, again with the few exceptions that spoil most generalizations – Sparta, which occupied Messenia, or Syracuse and Acragas, which swallowed neighbouring territories in Sicily.

The Greeks themselves had no hesitation, however, in calling Sparta or Syracuse a *polis*, the latter even though it was ruled by tyrants during much of the classical period when 'tyrant' and *polis* had come to have virtually contradictory connotations. Nor did they deny the term to those backward regions in which political organization and the civilization itself were still so rudimentary that they were admittedly more like that of the *Iliad* than like their contemporaries. In the old days, wrote Thucydides (I 5), piracy by land and sea was an honourable occupation among the Greeks as among the barbarians, and 'even today much of Hellas lives in the ancient manner: the Ozolian Locrians and the Aetolians and the Acarnanians and others in that part of the mainland'. And of course the word *polis* did not distinguish the structure of government; it implied nothing about democracy or oligarchy or even tyranny, no more than does 'state'.

Loose as the usage may have been at times, it never passed beyond certain limits. Its further extension was to equate *polis* with any independent Greek community (or one which had temporarily lost its independence). *Polis* was not applied to a league of states, no matter how voluntary the alliance; nor to a district like Arcadia which had a sort of autonomous (if abstract) existence, held together by common myths, dialect and cult, but which was not a political organism; nor, except very rarely, to barbarian states. All these, in Greek eyes, were, each in its own way, something essentially different from the true political community, and size was no unimportant part of the difference. They looked upon their compactness in territory and numbers not as a mere accident of history or geography but as a virtue. In Aristotle's words (*Politics* VII 1326b), 'A state composed of too many . . . will not be a true *polis* because it can hardly have a true constitution. Who can be the general of a mass so excessively large? And who can be herald, except Stentor?' The *polis* was not a place, though it occupied a defined territory; it was people acting in concert, and therefore they must be able to assemble and deal with problems face to face. That was a necessary condition, though not the only one, of self-government.

Ideally, self-sufficiency was another condition of genuine independence. It was admitted that this could rarely be achieved, if ever, because material resources were not evenly distributed (it is enough to mention iron), but, within the limits imposed by nature, much could be accomplished towards that objective. How much depended partly on size again – the *polis* must not be so small that it lacked the manpower to carry on the various activities of a civilized existence, including the requirements of defence. Given adequate numbers, the problem was one of proper rules of conduct and proper organization of social life. And there agreement stopped. The Athenian answer and the Spartan answer were radically different. Within Athens – using that city-state only as an example – there was no single answer either, hence the long complicated political debate which went on there.

That debate was conducted within a small closed circle inside the total population, for the *polis* was an exclusive community. In the middle of the fifth century the Athenians adopted a law restricting citizenship to the legitimate children of marriages in which both parents were themselves of citizen stock. This was an extreme measure, probably neither rigidly enforced for very long nor frequently repeated in other states, but the thinking behind it was fairly typical. There had been a time, only two or three generations earlier, when Greek aristocrats often arranged marriages for their children outside the community, sometimes even with barbarians (but then only on the level of chieftains). Pericles was a descendant in the fourth generation of an external alliance, his great-grandmother having been the daughter of the then tyrant of Sicyon; while his political opponent Cimon was the grandson on his mother's side of a Thracian king named Olorus. Now, under Pericles, Athens declared all such marriages illegal, their offspring bastards.

In a sense, the word 'citizen' is too weak, though technically correct; it does not – at least in our day – carry the full weight implicit in being a member of a *polis*-community. And if one were not born into the community it was nearly impossible to get in at all. There was no routine naturalization procedure, not even in a state like Athens which welcomed immigrants from other Greek cities, gave them considerable freedom and opportunity and accepted them socially. Only by formal action of the sovereign assembly could an outsider become a citizen of Athens, and the evidence is that very special considerations were necessary before the assembly could be persuaded. It was not enough, for example, to have been born in Athens, to serve in her armies and to behave decently and loyally, if one's parents were not citizens. Needless to say, more xenophobic states were, if anything, even more closed in. To open the doors wide was a sign of some deficiency, and it is more than coincidental that by the end of the fourth century some city-states were driven to sell citizenship in order to raise funds, precisely in the period when the classical *polis* was a declining, not to say dying, organism.

In the more urban and more cosmopolitan city-states in particular, therefore, a minority constituted the community proper. The majority included the non-citizens (the word 'foreigners' is best avoided, since most of them were Greeks), of whom the permanent residents were called 'metics' in Athens and some other places; the slaves, a still more numerous class; and, in a fundamental sense, all the women. Whatever their rights – and that was entirely in the power of the state – they suffered various disabilities as compared with the citizens, and at the same time they were fully subject to the authority of the state in which they resided. In that respect their position was no different from that of the citizens, for in principle the power of the Greek *polis* was total: it was the source of all rights and obligations, and its authority reached into every sphere of human behaviour without exception. There were things a Greek state customarily did not do, such as provide higher education or control interest rates, but even then its *right* to interfere was not in question. It merely chose not to. The *polis* was inescapable.

The question then arises, if the *polis* had such limitless authority, in what sense were the Greeks free men, as they believed themselves to be. Up to a point their answer was given in the epigram, 'The law is king'. Freedom was not equated with anarchy but with an ordered existence within a community which was governed by an established code respected by all. That was what had been fought for through much of the archaic period, first against the traditional privilege and monopoly of power possessed by the nobility, then against the unchecked power of the tyrants. The fact that the community was the sole source of law was a guarantee of freedom. On that all could agree, but the translation of the principle into practice was another matter; it brought the classical Greeks up against a difficulty which has persisted in political theory without firm resolution ever since. How free was the community to alter its established laws? If the laws could be changed at will, and that means by whichever faction or group held a commanding position in the state at any given moment, did that not amount to anarchy, to undermining the very stability and certainty which were implicit in the doctrine that the law was king?

So put, the problem is too abstract. In real life the answer normally depended on the interests of the respective protagonists. The sixth century saw the emergence in many communities of the common people as a political force, and against their demand for a full share in government there was promptly raised the defence of the sanctity of the law, of a code which, though it now recognized every citizen's right to a fair trial, to a minor share in government perhaps, even to the ballot, and to other undeniably new and important features of social organization, nevertheless restricted high civil and military office, and therefore policy-making, to men of birth and wealth. *Eunomia*, the well-ordered state ruled by law, had once been a revolutionary slogan; now it stood for the *status quo*. The people replied with *isonomia*, equality of political rights, and since the people were numerically in the majority, *isonomia* led to *demokratia*. Whose law, in other words, was to be king?

The underlying trouble, of course, was that the sense of community, strong as it was, clashed with the gross inequality which prevailed among the members. Poverty was widespread, the material standard of life was low and there was a deep cleavage between the poor and the rich, as every Greek writer concerned with politics knew and said. This has been common enough in all history; what gave it an uncommon twist in Greece was the city-state, with its intimacy, its stress on the community and on the freedom and dignity of the individual which went with membership. The citizen felt he had claims on the community, not merely obligations to it, and if the régime did not satisfy him he was not loath to do something about it – to get rid of it if he could. In consequence the dividing-line between politics and sedition (*stasis* the Greeks called it) was a thin one in classical Greece, and often enough *stasis* grew into ruthless civil war.

The classic description of extreme *stasis* is Thucydides' account of the singularly brutal outbreak in Corcyra in 427, treated by the historian explicitly as a model of this chronic evil in Greek society. Nothing reveals the depths of the bitterness better than the fact that both sides appealed to the slaves for support. Thucydides explained the phenomenon psychologically, as having its roots in human nature. It was Aristotle who tied it more closely, and very simply, to the nature and idea of the *polis*. 'Speaking generally,' he said in the *Politics* (V 1301b), 'men turn to *stasis* out of a desire for equality.' By its nature the *polis* awoke this desire, which men then had difficulty in achieving. Hence the bitterness of factional strife, the comparative frequency and virulence of civil war. There were exceptions, important ones – notably Athens and to a degree Sparta – but the rough generalization may be made that in the Greek *polis* it was not so much policy which caused the most serious divisions, but the question of who should rule, 'the few' or 'the many'. And always the question was complicated by external affairs, by war and imperial ambitions.

War and Empire

Because of their geographical situation the mainland Greeks were for a long time free from direct foreign pressure or attack. Not so, however, the settlements to the east and west. Apart from frequent troubles with more primitive people, like the Scythians to the north or the Thracians to the west of the Black Sea, there was the more serious matter of the powerful civilized empires. In Asia Minor the Greek cities came under the suzerainty of the Lydians in the sixth century, and then under the Persians. In Sicily they were repeatedly invaded by Carthage, which maintained a toehold on the western end of the island but never succeeded in conquering the rest.★

Persian rule meant annual payment of tribute, which was sizeable but in no sense crushing, passivity in foreign affairs, and economic and cultural freedom. Where Persia impinged most on the internal life of the Greek states was in her backing of tyrants, and this ultimately led to revolt, which broke out in 500 or 499, under circumstances which are far from clear. The Ionians immediately asked the mainland Greeks for help and received none, except for twenty ships from the recently established Athenian democracy and five more from Eretria in Euboea. Even so, it took Persia the better part of a decade to regain complete control, and she followed up her success with two massive invasions of Greece itself, the first in 490 sent by King Darius, the second in 480 under his successor, Xerxes.

Many communities followed their refusal to help the Ionian revolt by surrendering in fright to the invaders – 'Medizers' they were contemptuously called thereafter – and even the Delphic oracle played an equivocal role, at best. The Spartans, backed by the Peloponnesian League, had the only powerful army on the Greek side, but partly because of difficulties at home, partly because of a false strategic conception, they were dilatory in defence, though they proved what they could do, when tested, at Thermopylae and later at Plataea. It remained for Athens to deliver the most significant blows, at Marathon in 490 and off Salamis in 480. The latter was a most remarkable affair: persuaded by Themistocles, the Athenians hurriedly enlarged their fleet, withdrew from the city when the

★ Rome did not become a factor until about 300 B.C.

Persians came and allowed it to be destroyed, and then with their allies, smashed the invaders in a great sea-battle. The power of Athens, and therefore the history of classical Greece, henceforth rested on control of the sea.

The Persians were badly beaten; they were far from crushed. It was generally assumed that they would return for a third attempt (that in the end they did not was largely the result of troubles within their empire, which could not safely be forecast). Ordinary prudence therefore required combined anticipatory measures, and since they had to be taken in the Aegean and on the Asia Minor coast, rather than on the Greek mainland, it was natural that the leadership should be given to Athens. A league was organized under Athenian hegemony, with its administrative centre on the island of Delos (therefore historians call it the Delian League). Planned by the Athenian Aristeides on a system of contributions either in ships and sailors or in money, the League within a decade or so cleared the Persian fleet from the Aegean. As the danger lifted, the old desire for complete autonomy began to reassert itself, but Athens would not allow withdrawal from the League and forcibly put down any 'revolt'. So the League became an Empire, and the symbol of the change was the transfer of its headquarters and treasury in 454 from Delos to Athens. All but three of the member-states now contributed money and not ships, which meant that Athens provided, manned and controlled virtually the whole fleet herself. An indication of the magnitude of the annual tribute is that it approximately equalled the Athenian public revenue from internal sources.

For the next quarter-century the Athenian Empire was the most important single fact in Greek affairs, and Pericles was the dominant figure in Athenian affairs. His policy was expansionist, though highly controlled and disciplined. He greatly strengthened Athenian connexions in Thrace and southern

Russia, which had strategic significance but were above all important as the main source of Athens' vital corn imports; he made alliances with Sicilian cities; he tried, unsuccessfully, to attack Egypt; he came to terms with Persia. But Athenian relations with Sparta were increasingly difficult. Friendly at least in a formal way in the years following the Persian Wars, the two power blocks came into open conflict in the 450s, with some actual fighting, and then returned to a state of uneasy peace which lasted another two decades. Two major incidents involving Corinthian spheres of influence, at Corcyra and Potidaea, then precipitated the Peloponnesian War, which lasted with interruptions from 431 to 404, ending in the total defeat of Athens and the dissolution of her empire. Corinth may have been the chief advocate of war on the Spartan side, but, as the war's historian Thucydides wrote (I 23, 6), 'The growth of the power of Athens, and the alarm which this inspired in Sparta, made war inevitable.' Pericles probably thought so too, for he had been accumulating a large cash reserve, a most uncommon practice among Greek states, who customarily spent all their income quickly.

It seems to have taken Thucydides a long time to make up his mind about the underlying cause of the Peloponnesian War; more precisely, that there was a deep cause, as distinct from one or more triggering incidents. This was one of his boldest and most original conceptions. War, everyone recognized, was part of life. Plato opened his last and longest work, the *Laws,* with praise of the ancient 'lawgiver' of Crete for the way in which he prepared the community for war, 'since throughout life all must for ever sustain a war against all other *poleis*'. This may be rhetorical exaggeration; it is not Platonic irony. War was a normal instrument of policy which the Greeks used fully and frequently. They did not particularly seek war – the heroic ideals of the Homeric poems had been thoroughly damped down – but neither did they go to lengths to avoid it. In the fourth century, to be sure, there were signs of war-weariness and even talk of a 'common peace' within Hellas. Nothing came of this, however, and the individual states went right on quarrelling, blaming others when war came and justifying their own actions simply in terms of political necessity. The interests of the state were always justification enough, whether of war or of diplomacy and negotiation or of capitulation (if necessary, even to the Persians). The choice of instruments in any given situation was arguable only on the question of tactics, pragmatically but not morally.

The immediate causes of war were therefore as varied as the policies and interests of the different states, as the objectives they were pursuing at any given time. The desire for power and aggrandizement, border incidents, material enrichment through booty (with human chattels high on the list), protection of corn supply and transport, the search for outside support for internal faction – these all came into play, intensified by the fragmentation of Hellas, which had the effect of multiplying the number of independent, or would-be independent, states rubbing against each other. What was rare as a motive, however, was either trade, in the sense of a struggle over sea lanes and markets, like the Anglo-Dutch wars, for example, or territorial expansion, the direct incorporation of conquered land or its economic exploitation (other than by the collection of tribute).

Both the casualness of armed hostility and the way in which typical motives could be combined and at the same time create a conflict of interests is nicely illustrated in one particular situation in the Peloponnesian War. In 426 the Spartans settled a colony, for a number of reasons connected with the war, at Heraclea in Trachis, near the sea a few miles from the pass of Thermopylae. The colony was in trouble at once, because, Thucydides says (III 93, 2), 'the Thessalians, who were in control of that area, . . . feared that it would be a very powerful neighbour and they continually harassed and made war upon the new settlers'. The Thessalians, a loose federation of tribes, were in fact allied with Athens, yet Thucydides fails to give that as the ground for their hostility to Heraclea. His reasons do not emerge for some pages, until he comes to the year 424 and the campaigns of the Spartan general Brasidas, who set out for the north with 1,700 hoplites to carry the war into Thrace. Arriving in Heraclea, Brasidas 'sent a messenger to his friends in Pharsalus [a Thessalian town] asking them to conduct him and his army through the territory'. His 'friends' included a number of the leading oligarchs, and they did as he requested. 'The majority of Thessalian citizens', Thucydides then explains (IV 78), 'had always been favourable to the Athenians. Had there been genuine constitutional government in Thessaly rather than the customary rule by a narrow clique, Brasidas would never have been able to proceed.' As it was, he rushed through just in time, before the opposition were sufficiently mobilized to stop him. Thus, it was the interests of internal faction which decided policy, rather than the obligations of a formal external alliance. And there is no reason not to believe Thucydides that the Thessalians made war against Heraclea simply because a strong neighbour was someone to fear.

On the other hand, since war was a means and not an end, peaceful alternatives were also tried, and they did not always fail. It was power, in the end, which was the strongest force for peace – earlier the power of the tyrants, now the power of a few great city-states. Their superior ability to wage war was reinforced by a general realization that they would do so promptly if required. By itself no Greek state could generate that much power, but if one were big enough to begin with, persistent enough, sufficiently unified and under competent leadership, it could create and wield a power block. Alliances were valuable above all because they provided the leading states with auxiliary manpower. And in the pre-gunpowder world it was usually the weight of properly trained and equipped men which decided battles; among the Greeks, the heavy-armed hoplite infantry. Partly, therefore, peace was the result of simple arithmetic. Towards the end of the sixth century, for example, Sparta succeeded in bringing under alliance most of the free states of the Peloponnese. Some needed pressure, others did not, but who could say that the latter were more willing rather than just more cautiously calculating? Thereafter war among the Peloponnesian states was very rare indeed, until Thebes smashed Spartan power in 371. That blow at once proved to be a mixed blessing even to those who detested Sparta: it brought about the emancipation of the Messenian helots, but it also led to a holocaust of *stasis* and petty warfare all over the peninsula. The sums had been changed, so to speak, and war therefore returned, occupying the newly created power vacuum.

What modern historians call the Peloponnesian League was known to contemporaries by the more awkward, but revealing, name of 'Sparta and her allies'. The point is that there was a network of treaties tying each of the 'member states' to Sparta, and only the loosest sort of league organization under the hegemony of Sparta. This was a significant distinction, preserving the individual state's image of its autonomy. In an alliance it could pretend to be an equal, still a fully independent entity retaining its sovereign freedom of action; in a league it could be outvoted and lose control over its own actions. The reality did not coincide with the image, of course: states were rarely equals and bargaining between them was rarely free, and on the other hand even Sparta could not effectively mobilize the support of her allies without consulting them and obtaining their approval of the proposed course of action. Nevertheless, the myth of independence was so compelling that genuine leagues in Greek history were restricted either to the amphictyonies, which organized and shared control of certain pan-Hellenic shrines like Delphi; or to the most backward areas where the *polis* never came to life; or to the peculiar and complicated instance of the Boeotian League in which one powerful member, Thebes, sought domination in her own interest, and paid for her insistence by having to fight her neighbours over and over again.

The Boeotian League exposed the thinness of the line that separated allies from subjects, but it was the Athenian Empire, with an effective membership of more than 150 states in Asia Minor, the Hellespontine region, Thrace and the Aegean islands, which brought that issue to a head in classical Greece. After 454 there was no pretence about it: membership was compulsory and secession prohibited; members paid an annual cash tribute which was fixed, collected and spent by Athens at her sole discretion; these imperial resources enabled Athens to conduct a complicated foreign policy, which she alone determined; and there was a growing tendency for the Athenians to interfere in the internal affairs of the member-states, in particular to support and strengthen democratic elements against their oligarchic opponents. Some contemporaries began to refer to the 'tyrant city', a reproach which is readily repeated by historians today, chiefly on the authority of Thucydides. Yet that is far too one-sided a judgement; it looks only at the question of *polis* autonomy and ignores other, by no means meaningless, desires and values. Thucydides himself noted the friendliness to Athens among the majority of citizens in Thessaly, and the evidence suggests that the same was widely true among communities in the Empire. In the unending struggle between the few and the many Athens usually came down on the side of the many, who often needed such aid to maintain their position, and who therefore felt that tribute and some loss of autonomy were a price well worth paying in return for democratic government at home and peace abroad.

The decisive test came in the Peloponnesian War, in which few Greek states escaped some involvement except those on the outermost fringes of Hellas. This was a war quite without precedent in every respect, in the number of participants (both numbers of states and numbers of men), in its duration and therefore in the expenditure of resources and in the pressure on morale, in the crucial importance of sea power, and in the way in which the scene of actual fighting moved all over the place, from Asia Minor to Sicily, often in several widely dispersed areas simultaneously. It was a war which had therefore to be played by ear, as neither statesmen nor commanders had adequate precedents from which to learn. Ever since the invention of the massed hoplite formation, Greek wars were customarily shortlived affairs in the summer months, culminating in a single infantry engagement between the heavy armour on both sides, numbering in the hundreds or thousands. Eventually one side or the other broke and fled, and the battle – and usually the war – was over. The enemy was also harassed by raiding of crops, occasionally by a siege, usually unsuccessful unless treason took over, or by cavalry movements – but the encounter of the hoplites was normally the one decisive action. Hence there was no occasion for deep strategy, little need for financial preparations, nothing that one could seriously call logistics.

But these were wars between single states, with or without the support of a handful of allies, having an obvious battle terrain in which to contend. The Peloponnesian War involved great blocks of states and a wide choice of battle areas with little chance for a decision so long as the two centres, Sparta and Athens, remained intact. It was Pericles' idea not to risk a decision on the hoplite engagement, even at the expense of allowing the Spartans to raid Attica repeatedly without resistance. He counted on Athenian financial resources, on her peerless navy, and on her intangible psychological superiority.

In a word, he had a strategic idea, if not a plan, of considerable complexity, and its foundation was the solidity of the Empire. He was not wrong. Whatever the explanation for the ultimate defeat of Athens, it was not eagerness in the Empire to be released from the Athenian yoke. Naturally enough, both sides found in the course of twenty-seven years a very considerable unevenness in the reliability of their allies, and both sides did what they could to unhinge the alliances, using force, cajolement and, most effective of all, support for *stasis*. Brasidas was not alone in having 'friends' in the allied states of the other camp. The important thing about the Athenian Empire is not that there were defections, but that so much support continued to come to the 'tyrant city', even in the final decade when all seemed lost and one might have expected elementary *raison d'état* to drive her subjects to a quick bargain with the enemy.

In truth there is no simple and obvious explanation why Athens lost, and it is necessary to remember that she almost escaped. The peace of 421 was a victory in the restricted sense that not one of the main Spartan objectives was achieved. Then came the renewal of the war and in 415 the Athenians decided on a major stroke, the invasion of Sicily. It ended in a complete disaster, and though the war dragged on for another nine years, that defeat was clearly the turning-point. Yet it was a defeat by a hair's breadth; more competent leadership would almost certainly have turned the invasion into a success, with consequences that cannot be realistically guessed at, though they surely should not be underestimated. This failure of leadership, it is widely held on the inevitable authority of Thucydides, was symptomatic of a very deep and general decline in Athenian political behaviour after the death of Pericles in the second year of the war, and that is probably the commonest explanation of Athens' defeat. Perhaps, but it is at least arguable that this was a war Athens could lose but could not really win, simply because – given its size, its resources in men and materials, the incapacity of its rudimentary economy and technology to expand, and the incapacity of the Greeks either to transcend the *polis*, or, in most instances, to live at peace with themselves within it – final victory would have come to Athens only if she succeeded in bringing all Hellas within her empire, and that was apparently beyond reach.

The war ended in 404, and the most important condition laid down by the victorious Spartans was the dissolution of the Empire. The war was therefore a disaster not only for Athens but for all Greece: it disrupted the one possible road towards some kind of political unification, though admittedly a unity imposed on others by an ambitious city. Sparta fought the war under the slogan of restoring to the Greek cities their freedom and autonomy, and she honoured that aim first by effectively returning the Asia Minor Greeks to Persian suzerainty (in payment for Persian gold, without which she was unable to bring the war to a close); then by attempting to establish a tribute-paying empire of her own, with military governors and garrisons, on the corpse of the Athenian Empire. That incompetent effort did not last a decade. In the fourth century the power vacuum in Greece became a permanent condition, despite the efforts of Sparta, Thebes and Athens in turn to assert some sort of hegemony. The final answer was given by no Greek state but by Macedon under Philip II and his son Alexander.

Athens

It has been estimated that a third or slightly more of the citizens of Athens lived in the urban districts at the outbreak of the Peloponnesian War in 431, a proportion which a century later had risen to perhaps one half. The free non-citizens, barred by law from owning land, were concentrated in the city and the harbour-town. So were many of the slaves. The purely demographic consequence was that Athens and the Piraeus were each more populous than a majority of Greek states taken whole. This urban quality of Athenian life was of the greatest importance, a necessary condition for the power and much of the glory of the state. Nevertheless, the tenacity of the attachment to the soil must not be overlooked. The urban dwellers included no small number whose economic interest, in whole or in part, remained in the land. There is evidence that even at the end of the fifth century three-quarters of the citizen families owned some landed property, though not always enough for a livelihood. Of these it would be the wealthier, in particular, who resided in the city. As for the countrymen proper, when they were all brought behind the walls in the summer of 431, in anticipation of the first of the Spartan incursions, 'they were depressed', Thucydides reports (II 16, 2), 'and they bore with bitterness having to leave their homes and hereditary shrines'.

In the city were some hundreds of families of outstanding wealth: citizens living on the income from their estates and, occasionally, on investment in slaves; non-citizens whose economic base was trade or manufacture or money-lending. In a few cases it is possible to get an idea of the scale. Pericles' chief political opponent in his earlier years was Cimon, a member of one of the greatest of the old aristocratic families, and he, according to Aristotle (*Const. of Athens*, XXVII 3), 'possessed the fortune of a tyrant, . . . supported many of his fellow-demesmen, every one of whom was free to come daily and receive from him enough for his sustenance. Besides, none of his estates was enclosed, so that anyone who wished could take from its fruits'. Or there was Nicias, commander of the army destroyed in Sicily, who is reported to have owned 1,000 slaves; or the man, whose very name is unknown, who itemized in court his personal contributions to the navy and to the cost of public festivals in the final seven years of the Peloponnesian War, totalling nearly eleven talents, the equivalent of a year's wages for well over 200 skilled workmen.

The rich were essentially rentiers, free to devote themselves to politics or learning or plain idling. This was as true of Nicias as of the absentee landlords, for Nicias did not employ his slaves directly, but hired them out on a *per diem* rental to entrepreneurs holding concessions in the silver mines at Laurium. Even those who, like Cleon, made use of their slaves in their own industrial establishments, and therefore cannot be called rentiers in a strict sense, were (or, at least, could be if they wished) no less men of leisure; their businesses were managed in the same fashion as large landed estates, by slave bailiffs or foremen. The exact number of slaves in Athens is in dispute; it may be doubted if any contemporary could have given the figure, in the absence of either a register or a periodic census. Probably 60,000–80,000 is a fair estimate, which is about the same proportion of the total population of the state as prevailed in the American South before the Civil War. The heaviest concentrations were in the mines and in domestic service, the latter a broad category including thousands of unproductive men and women retained by men of means because it was the thing to do. Plato, for example, mentioned five domestics in his will, Aristotle more than fourteen, his successor, Theophrastus, seven. In agriculture and manufacture the slaves were fewer in number, and they were outnumbered in these branches of the economy by the free peasants and probably also by the free, independent craftsmen. Nevertheless, it was in these productive areas that the significance of slaves was perhaps the greatest, because they released from any economic concern, or even activity, the men who gave political leadership to the state, and in large measure the intellectual leadership as well.

The overwhelming mass of the Athenians, whether they owned a slave or two or not, found themselves largely occupied with procuring a livelihood, and many never rose above the minimum standard. There were many poor families in the countryside, and there were probably even more in the town. Nevertheless, in the classical period Athens remained free from the chronic Greek troubles arising out of a depressed and often dispossessed peasantry. Furthermore, even the poor often found both time and the opportunity to participate in the public life of the community, both in government (broadly defined) and in the rich festival activity associated with the cults of the state. How these exceptional patterns of behaviour came into being is one of the central questions in Athenian history.

Part of the answer can be found in the distribution of the military burdens and obligations. When the war with Sparta became a fact, Pericles personally led a great invasion – more properly it can be called a demonstration or parade – into the territory of Megara with 13,000 hoplites, 10,000 of them citizens, the rest metics. Another 3,000 were at that moment engaged in the siege of Potidaea, and the evidence suggests that the two groups together made up the full hoplite force in 431, or very nearly so. (Army figures cited by a writer such as Thucydides, unlike general population figures, are apt to be accurate: Greek states conducted no censuses but for obvious reasons they kept reliable registers of their armed forces, and these could be consulted by any citizen in a state such as Athens.) The total number of adult male citizens at that time was of the order of 40,000–45,000; therefore about one-third of the citizens (ignoring the metics in this calculation) had sufficient means to be classed as hoplites. Granted that those just above the minimum qualification may have found this a hardship, as those just below might well have thanked their good fortune for their narrow escape, the proportion still offers a useful indication of the spread of wealth in the state.

Every citizen and metic was liable for military service, the size of any given levy being determined by the Assembly. Most commonly, however, only the hoplites and cavalry, that is, the two wealthier sectors, were called out. They were required to provide and maintain their own equipment, and they received from the state nothing more than a *per diem* allowance while on duty (in the fourth century, when the treasury could not stand the strain, often not even that). Although the so-called light-armed levies were occasionally summoned to duty, it remains accurate to say that in Athens the army, conscript and not professional in any modern sense, was strictly an upper- and middle-class institution. The navy, in contrast, was altogether different, and differently organized. Command of the vessels was distributed among the richer citizens, who were also responsible for a considerable share of the operating costs, while the crews were paid professionals. Much of the detail remains very obscure, but it seems probable that some 12,000 men were so engaged normally up to eight months in the year. Although the citizen-body could not have supplied anything like that number, there were enough of them to constitute a very significant element. For the urban poor, the navy was a most important source of livelihood, at least while the Athenian Empire existed, a fact which was perfectly visible to every contemporary, as were its political implications. 'It is the *demos*', wrote an anonymous fifth-century pamphleteer commonly and too amiably referred to as the Old Oligarch, 'which drives the boats and gives the state its strength.'

Now *demos* was a word with a complicated history. The Old Oligarch used it in its sense of the 'common people', the 'lower classes', with the pejorative overtones proper to all right-thinking men as far back as the *Iliad*. But *demos* also meant the 'people as a whole'; in a democracy, the citizen-body who acted through their Assembly. Hence decrees of the Athenian Assembly were passed, in the official language of the documents, 'by the *demos*' rather than 'by the *ecclesia*' (the Greek word for 'assembly'). The Assembly met frequently – at least four times in every thirty-six-day period in the fourth century and perhaps as often in the fifth – and every male citizen who had reached his eighteenth birthday was eligible to attend whenever he chose, barring a few who had lost their civic rights for one offence or another. Obviously a mere fraction of the 40,000 came, but those who were present at any single meeting were the *demos* on that occasion, and their acts were recognized, in law, as the actions of the whole people. Then, by a curious extension of this principle, it was held that the jury-courts, selected by lot from a panel of 6,000 men, volunteers from among all the citizens, were also equal to the whole *demos* in matters which fell within their competence.

Direct participation was the key to Athenian democracy: there was neither representation nor a civil service or bureaucracy in any significant sense. In the sovereign Assembly, whose authority was essentially total, every citizen was not only entitled to attend as often as he pleased but he also had the right to enter the debate, offer amendments and vote on the proposals, on war and peace, taxation, cult regulation, army levies, war finance, public works, treaties and diplomatic negotiations, and anything else, major or minor, which required governmental decision. Much of the preparatory work for these meetings was done by the *boule*, a Council of 500 chosen by lot for one year – and again everyone was eligible, save that no man could be a member more than twice in his lifetime. Then there were a large number of officials, of varying importance, most of them also designated by lot for one year: the few exceptions included the ten generals (*strategoi*), who were elected and could be re-elected without limit, and temporary *ad hoc* commissions for diplomatic negotiation and the like. There was no hierarchy among the offices; regardless of the significance or insignificance of any post, every holder was responsible directly and solely to the *demos* itself, in the Council or the Assembly or the courts, and not to a superior officeholder.

This system was, of course, the product of a considerable evolution, completed in its essentials by the third quarter of the fifth century, but subject to further modification as long as Athens remained a democracy. The Athenians sometimes called Solon the father of their democracy, but that was an anachronistic myth. Although both Solon and Peisistratus in different ways laid some of the groundwork by weakening the archaic system, especially the political monopoly of the aristocratic families, neither man, it need hardly be said, had democracy in view. The change, when it came, was sharp and sudden, following the overthrow of the tyranny in 510 with Spartan help and a two-year civil war which ensued; and the architect of the new type of government was Cleisthenes, a member of the noble family of the Alcmaeonids. Cleisthenes was no theorist, and he seems to have become a democrat virtually by accident, turning to the common people when he urgently needed their support in the confused struggle to fill the vacuum left by the deposed tyrant, Hippias the son of Peisistratus. We are too ill informed to say how much of a model for his new set-up Cleisthenes was able to find elsewhere in Greece, in Chios, for example, but the final result was in any case original in the best Greek sense. Having committed himself to a major innovation, Cleisthenes with his advisers, whoever they may have been, created the institutions which they thought their new objective required, retaining what they could, but not hesitating to demolish and to invent boldly and radically.

The Cleisthenic structure was not yet the Periclean: two

full generations were required to perfect the system, a period which included not only the Persian Wars and the building of the Empire but also much internal conflict, for the forces opposed to democracy were far from crushed in 508. The details of that struggle can no longer be retraced with any clarity; of all the gaps in our knowledge of classical Greek history this is perhaps the most frustrating. The man who played the decisive role between Cleisthenes and Pericles was Ephialtes, and we know next to nothing about him or his career. He was assassinated in 462 or 461, a political crime which passed almost unnoticed in Greek literature, and that silence is sufficient commentary on the tendentiousness of Greek writers, a one-sidedness with which the modern historian must grapple all the time, and never more than in the study of the history and functioning of the Athenian democracy.

In the end the pivotal mechanisms were election by lot, which translated equality of opportunity from an ideal to a reality; and pay for office, which permitted the poor man to sit on the Council and jury-courts or to hold office when the lot fell to him. It was not without reason that Pericles could boast, according to Thucydides, that it was one of the positive peculiarities of Athens that poverty was no bar to public service. When one adds up the Assembly, the Council, the courts and the large number of rotating offices, the total – several thousands – indicates a direct participation in the work of government widely shared among the citizen-body, an uncommon degree of political experience cutting right across the class structure. The distribution was, of course, not an even one: that would have been too utopian. In particular, the rural population was probably under-represented in ordinary circumstances, and at the top, among the men who gave the leadership and formulated policy, very few are known (and they not before the fourth century) to have come from the lower classes.

In a sense, amateurism was implicit in the Athenian 'definition' of a direct democracy. Every citizen was held to be qualified to share in government by the mere fact of his citizenship, and his chances to play a part were much intensified not only by the wide use of the lot but also by the compulsory rotation in the Council and most offices. Though the pay was sufficient to compensate a man for the wages he might have lost as a craftsman or labourer, it was no higher than that. Hence no man could count on office-holding as a regular livelihood, or even as a better one for some periods of his life. At the same time, a large state like Athens, with its Empire and its (by Greek standards) complex fiscal, naval and diplomatic affairs, absolutely needed full-time politicians to guide and coordinate the work of the more or less temporary amateur participants. And it found them among the men of wealth, the rentiers who were free to devote themselves wholly to public affairs. Down to the Peloponnesian War these men were apparently drawn entirely from the old landed families. Then new men broke their monopoly – Cleon, Cleophon, Anytus – whose leisure was provided by slave craftsmen, and for the remaining century of democratic government in Athens the balance of leadership perhaps leaned more on that side, punctuated occasionally by really poor men who worked their way to the top, not without suspicion that monetary corruption played some part in their rise.

It became increasingly common to refer to these men as 'orators', almost as a technical term and not just as a description of their particular abilities in that direction. Because the Assembly alone made policy and held control, in conjunction with the courts, not only over the affairs of state but also over all officials, military or civil, leadership of the state lay in the Assembly. It met in the open, on a hill near the Acropolis called the Pnyx, where thousands gathered (just how many thousands is another frustrating unknown) to debate and decide. The Assembly, in a word, was a mass-meeting and to address it required, in the strictest sense, the power of oratory. Because it had no fixed composition, because no one was chosen to attend, it had no political parties or 'government', nor any other principle of organization. The president for the day was chosen by lot from the members of the Council on the usual scheme of rotation, motions were made, argued and amended, and the vote was taken, all in a single sitting except in rare circumstances. Anyone who sought to guide it in its policy-making had to appear on the Pnyx and present his reasons. Neither the holding of office nor a seat on the Council was a substitute. A man was a leader so long, and only so long, as the Assembly accepted his programme in preference to those of his opponents.

Ancient critics and their modern followers have not been sparing in their condemnation: after Pericles, they say, the new type of leader was a demagogue, pandering to the *demos* in the Assembly and the courts at the expense of the higher interests of the state. No doubt not all the men who achieved political eminence in Athens were selfless altruists, and mass-meetings on the scale of those on the Pnyx invited emotional and even inflammatory speech-making. It would be odd, however, if dishonest politicians and excessive rhetoric were wholly unknown in the earlier years of the democracy, then to come on with a rush when Pericles died. Besides, there is enough evidence to suggest that the overall record and achievement of the Assembly remained creditable to the end. It is a fact that the state often followed a consistent line for rather long periods, in each instance identified with one individual or a small group. For all their experience, most citizens were unable to cope with the intricacies of finance or foreign affairs and tended, quite rightly, to give their support to those full-time politicians whom they trusted (and whom they could always check). Hence not only Pericles in the fifth century and Demosthenes late in the fourth were permitted to develop long-term policies, but also less famous, though far from untalented men like Thrasybulus or Eubulus in the intervening years.

It is also a fact that Athens never ran short of men of the highest ability who were willing to devote themselves to politics, though the rewards were largely honorific and the personal risks considerable. Conflict was often sharp, and the issues were serious and not just shadow-boxing for prestige or personal status. The long struggle to anchor the democracy itself, the growth of the Empire, the Peloponnesian War and its strategy, public finance and finally the question of Philip and Alexander – these were matters worthy of passion. And they were fought with passion. Whoever aspired to leadership could not do otherwise, and in a system lacking the buttressing and mediating institutions of party and bureaucracy, such men lived under constant tension. It is not surprising that they sometimes reacted violently, that they seized the occasion to crush an opponent; or that the *demos* was sometimes impatient with failure, real or imaginary. There was no immunity from the risks: even Pericles suffered temporary eclipse and a heavy fine early in the Peloponnesian War. Others were ostracized, sent into a kind of honorary exile for ten years, but without loss of property and without social disgrace. When ostracism was dropped as a practice near the end of the fifth century, ordinary exile on 'criminal charges' remained as a possibility. And a very few met death, legally or by assassination.

One could easily compile a catalogue of the cases of repression, sycophancy, irrational behaviour and outright brutality in the nearly two centuries that Athens was governed as a democracy. Yet they remained no more than so many single incidents in this long stretch of time when Athens was remarkably free from the universal Greek malady of sedition and civil war. Twice there were oligarchic coups, in 411 and 404, but they were short-lived, came under the severe stress of a war that was being lost, and the second time succeeded for a few months only because of the intervention of the victorious Spartan army. Thereafter no more is heard of oligarchy in Athens (outside the writings of some philosophers) until another invader, the Macedonians, closed this chapter of Greek history completely in 322. Not a few of the supporters of the 404 coup – known thereafter by the deservedly malodorous name of the Thirty Tyrants – had been active in the oligarchy of 411. That they lived to play their seditious role twice in a decade is not unworthy of note. Indeed, even so staunch a libertarian as John Stuart Mill thought this was perhaps too much.

The Athenian Many, of whose democratic irritability and suspicion we hear so much, are rather to be accused of too easy and good-natured a confidence, when we reflect that they had living in the midst of them the very men who, on the first show of an opportunity, were ready to compass the subversion of the democracy.

By the middle of the fifth century the 'few' and the 'many' among the Athenian citizens had established a satisfactory working balance, which is but another way of saying that they had achieved a system which was virtually *stasis*-proof. For the 'many' the state provided both significant material benefits and a very considerable share in government, for the 'few' – and they were a fairly numerous class – the honours and satisfactions that went with political and military leadership. Political success and economic prosperity served as unifying factors, making it possible to meet the enormous costs of office and the fleet, without which the participation, and even the loyalty, of thousands of the poorest citizens would have been uncertain at best; and providing powerful psychological stimuli to civic pride and close personal identification with the *polis*. Without the Empire it is hard to imagine the initial triumph of the system Ephialtes and Pericles forged. Then the system generated its own momentum, sustained by an active sense of civic responsibility – so that the wealthy, for example, carried a heavy burden of financial charges and the main military burden, while the *demos* accepted leadership from their ranks – and not even the disasters of the Peloponnesian War or the loss of the Empire seriously threatened the structure of government. Fourth-century Athens found resources within herself to maintain the political and civic organization which the Empire had helped erect in the previous century.

Athens prospered as did no other classical Greek state. The greatest of her boasts, attributed to Pericles, was that she was the 'school of Hellas'. In two centuries she produced an incredible succession of superb writers and artists, scientists and philosophers. Many who were not native, furthermore, were powerfully attracted to the city, and some of them settled there more or less permanently. There were not many important figures in Greek cultural life between the years 500 and 300 who were not associated with Athens for at least part of their career, including some of the bitterest critics of her system. None was more severe than Plato, a native Athenian who found much to admire in the state often held up as her ideal opposite, namely, Sparta. He and those who thought like him conveniently forgot that in Sparta they would never even have begun to think, let alone been permitted to teach freely as they did.

Sparta

It has been said that Sparta had two separate histories, its own and that of its image abroad (or 'mirage' as one French scholar calls it). Considering how much was written about Sparta in antiquity, it is remarkable how confused, contradictory and incomplete the picture is. Partly this is because the mirage is constantly cutting across the reality, distorting it and often concealing it altogether; and partly because the Spartans themselves were so completely silent. There was a time, in the archaic period, when Sparta played a leading part in the development of the main lines of Greek civilization: in poetry, as we know from the bits that still exist; in music, according to reliable ancient traditions; even, it seems, in sea-faring and in creating some of the germinal institutions of the city-state. After about 600, however, there was an apparently abrupt break. From then on, not a single Spartan citizen is remembered for any cultural activity. Their famed 'laconic speech' was a mark that they had nothing to say, the final consequence of the peculiar way of life they had brought to completion by this time.

In population Sparta did not rank with the bigger states. The largest number of Spartans ever to engage in battle, so far as we know, were the 5,000 at Plataea in 479. Thereafter they declined steadily, until in the mid-fourth century they could not muster 1,000 men. That figure is cited by Aristotle as a symptom of the defectiveness of their system, for, he argued, the territory under their control could support 1,500 cavalry and 10,000 infantry. By conquest Sparta held the districts of Laconia and Messenia, quite fertile by Greek standards, giving her access to the sea and supplying that rare and invaluable natural resource, iron (a fitting counterpart to the Athenian silver). What this territory supported was not a free population but subject peoples of two kinds. The helots were in outright servitude, a compulsory labour force working the land for the Spartans. Their number cannot even be guessed, but it was certainly many times that of the Spartans themselves. The others, known as *perioeci*, retained their personal freedom and their own community organization in return for surrendering all right of action to Sparta in the military and foreign fields.

Thus restricted, the communities of the *perioeci* were, strictly speaking, incomplete *poleis*; yet there is no sign that they struggled to free themselves from Spartan authority in the way the smaller Boeotian states persistently battled Theban efforts to establish an overlordship. No doubt resignation was the only prudent course, but other considerations were also present: peace, protection and economic advantage. It was the *perioeci* who managed the trade and industrial production for Spartan needs, and it was they who maintained Laconian ware on a respectable, and sometimes high, level of craftsmanship and artistry. The helots were an altogether different matter. The usual practice throughout most of antiquity, when a city or district was enslaved, was to sell off the inhabitants and disperse them. The Spartans, however, had adopted the dangerous alternative of keeping them in subjugation at home, in their native territory – and they paid the price. Whereas Greek history was astonishingly free from slave revolts, even where there were large concentrations as in the Attic silver mines, helot revolts were always smouldering and occasionally burst out in full flaming force.

What kept the helots enslaved and prevented still more frequent rebellion was the emergence of Sparta as an armed camp, a development to which the key lay in Messenia, conquered later than Laconia and much more thoroughly reduced (so much so that this district remained virtually empty of the great architectural works which everywhere else were the visible marks of Hellenism). Soon after the middle of the seventh century the Messenian helots revolted: tradition calls that conflict the Second Messenian War and gives it a duration of no less than seventeen years. The Messenians were finally crushed, and the lesson they taught was translated into a thorough social and constitutional reform, the establishment in its final form of the Spartan system, and ultimately of the Spartan mirage. Henceforth the Spartan citizen-body were a professional soldiery, bred from childhood for two qualities, military skill and absolute obedience, free from (indeed, barred from) all other vocational interests and activities, living a barrack life, always ready to take the field in strength against any foe, whether helot or outsider. Their needs were met by the helots and the *perioeci*; their training was provided by the state; their obedience was secured by their education and by a set of laws which tried to prevent economic inequality and any form of gainful pursuit. The whole system was closed in against outside influence, against outsiders in person and even against imported goods. No state could match Sparta in its exclusiveness or its xenophobia.

The governmental structure was often praised in antiquity for its 'mixed' character, supposedly providing a balance between monarchical, aristocratic and democratic elements. The two hereditary kings commanded the armies in the field and were members of the Council of Elders, the others, twenty-eight in number, being elected for life from among the citizens over sixty years of age. The Assembly included everyone, but its role seems to have been a rather passive one: it could neither initiate action nor amend proposals submitted to it; it could only approve or vote them down; and one may wonder how much independence of judgement was exercised by a body of men for whom strict military obedience was the paramount virtue. Most powerful of all were the five ephors, elected annually from all the citizens. They had a general supervisory position over the affairs of the state as well as important judicial functions.

Spartan discipline and Spartan military prowess – they were a professional army in a world of citizen militias and mercenary bands – elevated Sparta into a major power, far beyond what her size would otherwise have warranted. Her first and only unwavering concern was peace at home, in the Peloponnese. This she never fully achieved, but she came near enough through the instrumentality of the Peloponnesian League. The League gave Sparta military assistance, and it was this help, together with armies from among the *perioeci*, which built her strength, in numerical terms, to major proportions. In the sixth century Sparta became beyond question the greatest Greek military force on land, and her allies provided adequate naval support, too, until that arm was surpassed by the creation of the all-powerful Athenian fleet.

Yet the fact remains that from the Persian Wars on, Spartan history is one of decline, despite her coalition victory (aided by Persian gold) over Athens in 404. Her xenophobic society was marked by a steadily decreasing population, for she stubbornly refused to recruit new citizens even when the need for manpower became desperate, preferring to arm freed helots, all sorts of social outcasts and even mercenaries. The Peloponnesian War put unbearable pressure not only on manpower but also on leadership: continuous campaigning by numbers of armies had not been provided for in the system, and some of the new commanders, most notably Lysander, who achieved the final victory, revealed no virtues other than ruthless military competence tied to ugly personal ambition. Lack of vision and mental inflexibility, whether in politics or social matters, proved most ruinous in times of success. Even Sparta's famed egalitarianism turned out to be incomplete and finally unworkable. Kings and commanders quarrelled frequently, among themselves or with the ephors, and the suspicion seems justified that the disagreements were not merely over tactics or policy. Abroad they were quickly corrupted and unmanageable. The property system broke down, though we do not quite know how: an increasing number of Spartans lost their land allotments, held by them from the state and worked for them by helots, and with their land they automatically lost their status as full Spartiates. Others accumulated wealth, though that could only be done illegally.

Herodotus suggests the widespread accessibility of Spartans to bribery as early as the beginning of the fifth century, with their kings commanding the highest price.

The Sparta which won the Peloponnesian War proved to be far more hollow than any contemporary could reasonably have guessed. In another decade her balanced constitution and her *eunomia* failed, and *stasis* struck, though only briefly. Then came the defeat by Thebes in 371. Thereafter, though Sparta still played a role in Greek politics, it was as a ghost of past glory. In a real crisis – as Philip of Macedon saw – she was only a minor state, like hundreds of others, no longer a serious force in the real world. And in the third century, finally and ironically, she virtually blew up in one of the most virulent civil wars in all Greek history. But the myth of Sparta was nevertheless strong and tenacious. The brilliance of Athens must not blot out the fact that there were Greeks (and men in later ages, too) for whom Sparta was the ideal. She was the model of the closed society, admired by those who reject an open society with its factional politics, its acceptance of the *demos* as a political force, its frequent 'lack of discipline', its recognition of the dignity and claims of the individual.

The Decline of the Polis

After the battle of Chaeronea in 338, Philip II of Macedon was effectively the master of Greece (excluding the Sicilian and other western Greeks). He then summoned all the states to a congress in Corinth, where a League of the Hellenes was founded, with the king as head and commander-in-chief, and with two objectives explicitly stated. One was an invasion of Persia on the remarkably thin pretext of getting revenge for the Persian desecration of Greek shrines 150 years earlier. The other was to employ the combined strength of the member-states to ensure, in the words of an anonymous writer later in the century (Pseudo-Demosthenes, XVII 15), that in no city-state 'shall there be execution or banishment contrary to the established laws of the *poleis*, nor confiscation of property, nor redistribution of land, nor cancellation of debts, nor freeing of slaves for purposes of revolution'.

No single action could have summed up more completely the change that had come over Greek politics. *Stasis* had always been a threat, and sometimes a bitter reality, but never before had it been possible, or even thinkable, that the other Greek states, including Athens, should organize to maintain the *status quo* as a matter of general policy, not to be confused with intervention by one state, usually a more powerful one, in the internal affairs of another to protect its own state interests. Relations with Persia had had a chequered history, but now, as Isocrates, the most persistent and straight-talking propagandist of the war-of-revenge programme, revealed on more than one occasion in his pamphlets, invasion of the Persian Empire was proposed as the only way to save Greece from itself: to provide a cause which would divert the Greeks from fighting each other, to provide booty with which to fill empty public treasuries, and to open up territory for emigration. And the saviour, the man under whose hegemony all these great things were to be accomplished, was a despot and an outsider, at best an 'honorary Hellene', whose own motives and interests, it need scarcely be said, were fundamentally not those of the Greeks he was to lead.

The success of Philip, repeated by his son Alexander, illustrated once again, and for the last time, the rule that the political difficulties which were rooted in the fragmentation of Hellas were susceptible only to an imposed solution, whether by a more powerful Greek state or by a powerful outsider. No one, not even the proponents of pan-Hellenic peace and coalition, suggested political integration of the city-states into larger units, for example. And no one was able to suggest, even hypothetically, how to overcome the poverty of natural resources and the low level of technology, except by moving out against Persia. Whenever in Greek history economic difficulties became critical, and that meant agrarian crisis, they were solved either by revolutionary means or by looking abroad, whether by emigration to new lands, as in the long colonization period, or by one or another form of pressure on other Greeks. Now, in the fourth century, the areas open to expansion abroad were severely restricted, and the relative weakness of the once great states gave much scope for intra-Hellenic warfare almost without end. Not even the sanctuaries were immune: in 356 the Phocians seized Delphi and used its treasure to hire a mercenary force of 10,000 and become for a fleeting moment the greatest military power in all Greece.

The available evidence suggests that in the period 399–375 there were never less than 25,000 Greek mercenaries in active service somewhere, and that later the figure rose to 50,000. The significance of these numbers is underscored by matching them against the low population figures as a whole, and by noticing how widely the mercenaries ranged, how indifferent they were to 'national' considerations in their search for employment. The century opened with the most famous of all Greek mercenary armies, the 'Ten Thousand' of Xenophon's *Anabasis*, who marched east on behalf of the younger brother of the Persian king in his unsuccessful attempt to seize the throne. In 343 we find another 10,000 Greeks – 1,000 from Thebes, 3,000 from Argos and 6,000 from Asia Minor – in the army with which the Persians recaptured Egypt for their Empire.

Nor were mercenaries the only footloose Greeks at the time. The number of political exiles was very large too, though they cannot be counted; the story is inherently improbable that 20,000 of them assembled at the Olympic Games in 324 to hear read out Alexander's decree ordering the Greek states to accept the return of all exiles, but there is no reason to suspect the figure itself as a clue to how many exiles there were to be dealt with under the decree. Many more exiles, furthermore, were established in new homes and had no wish to return to the old. In the years immediately before Chaeronea, for example, the Corinthian Timoleon, following a spectacular campaign to clear Sicily of tyrants, re-colonized a badly depleted Syracuse with volunteers from the Greek mainland and islands and even from Asia Minor. Tens of thousands apparently answered the call, some political exiles but no small number ordinary Greeks hoping to find a better livelihood.

All this movement, like the constant *stasis*, marked a failing of the community, and therefore of the *polis*. The more the *polis* had to hire its armed forces, the more citizens it could no longer satisfy economically, and that meant above all with land, so that they went elsewhere in order to live; the more it failed to maintain some sort of equilibrium between the few and the many, the more the cities were populated by out-siders, whether free migrants from abroad or emancipated slaves (who can be called metaphorically free migrants from within) – the less meaningful, the less real was the community. 'Decline' is a tricky and dangerous word to use in this con-text: it has biological overtones which are inappropriate, and it evokes a continuous downhill movement in all aspects of civilization which is demonstrably false. Yet there is no escap-ing the evidence: the fourth century was the time when the Greek *polis* declined, unevenly, with bursts of recovery and heroic moments of struggle to save itself, to become, after Alexander, a sham *polis* in which the preservation of many external forms of *polis* life could not conceal that hence-forth the Greeks lived, in Clemenceau's words, 'in the sweet peace of decadence, accepting all sorts of servitudes as they came'.

And again Athens was the exception. Her political system made extraordinary demands on the political skill and stability of her citizens and on their financial resources, which the loss of empire intensified many times over. It was no accident that several of her most important fourth-century leaders were experts in public finance, a theme which recurs persistently in the political speeches of Demosthenes. Or that so much diplomatic activity was concentrated on the Black Sea areas, where Athens was compelled to guarantee and protect her vital corn supplies by skill in diplomacy alone, now that she was no longer mistress of the Aegean in an imperial way. The final test was set by the Macedonians, and after years of understandable hesitation and debate the Athenian *demos* decided to fight for the independence of the *polis* (which is the same thing as saying the survival of the *polis*) and they almost succeeded. They failed and then the end came rapidly, symbolized in a single action, the handing over in 322 of Demosthenes and a number of his colleagues to the Macedonians for execution.

Yet even fourth-century Athens was not free from signs of the general decline. Contemporary political commentators themselves made much of the fact that whereas right through the fifth century political leaders were, and were expected to be, military leaders at the same time, so that among the ten generals were regularly found the outstanding political figures (elected to the office because of their political importance, not the other way round), in the fourth century the two sides of public activity, the civil and the military, were separated. The generals were now professional soldiers, most of them quite outside politics or political influence, who often served foreign powers as mercenary commanders as well as serving their own *polis*. There are a number of reasons for the shift, among which the inadequate finances of the state rank high, but, whatever the explanation, the break was a bad thing for the *polis*, a cleavage in the responsibility of the members to their community which weakened the sense of community without producing visibly better generalship. In the navy the signs took a different form. A heavy share of the costs still fell on the richest 1,200 men and the navy continued to perform well, but there was more evasion of responsibility, more need than before to compel the contributions and to pursue the defaulters at law. The crews themselves were often conscripted; voluntary enlistment could no longer provide the necessary complements. No doubt that was primarily because the treasury was too depleted to provide regular pay for long periods, just as the unwillingness of some to contribute their allotted share of the expenses resulted from an unsatisfactory system of distributing the burden, rather than from lack of patriotism. Wherever the responsibility lay, however, the result was again a partial breakdown in the *polis*.

There is no need to exaggerate: Athens nearly carried it off and the end came because Macedon, or at least Alexander, was simply too powerful. But Macedon did exist, and so did Persia and Carthage, and later Rome. The *polis* was developed in such a world, not in a vacuum or in Cloudcuckooland, and it grew on poor Greek soil. Was it really a viable form of political organization? Were its decline and disappearance the result of factors which could have been remedied, or of an accident – the power of Macedon – or of inherent structural weaknesses? These questions have exercised philosophers and historians ever since the late fifth century (and it is noteworthy how the problem was being posed long before the *polis* could be thought of as on its way out in any literal sense). Plato wished to rescue it by placing all authority in the hands of morally perfect philosophers. Others blame the *demos* and their mis-leaders, the demagogues, for every ill. Still others, especially in the past century or so, insist on the stupid failure to unite in a national state. For all their disparity, these solutions all have one thing in common: they all propose to rescue the *polis* by destroying it, by replacing it, in its root-sense of a community which is at the same time a self-governing state, by something else. The *polis*, one concludes, was a brilliant conception, but one which required so rare a combination of material and institutional circumstances that it could never be realized; that it could be approximated only for a very brief period of time; that it had a past, a fleeting present and no future. In that fleeting moment its members succeeded in capturing and recording, as man has not often done in his history, the greatness of which the human mind and spirit are capable.

CHAPTER 5

LITERATURE

In cities like Athens reading, writing and arithmetic appear to have been common attainments among the free population. Education was not the state's responsibility but a private one (unless one counts military training and the gymnasium), and until the middle of the fifth century formal teaching stopped at the elementary level. Vocational training, of course, was acquired in the home or through apprenticeship. Professional coaching was available in horsemanship, athletics and wrestling. But in literature or philosophy, men even of the generation of Pericles or Sophocles learned everything they knew by individual precept and informally from their elders and contemporaries, or by their own efforts. Then came the men known as 'sophists', who travelled to the main centres offering, for large fees, education in rhetoric, philosophy and statecraft. Advanced education grew from this initial impetus, remaining a private and expensive activity, usually on the basis of a master-disciple relationship.

Books consisted of sheets made from thin strips of an Egyptian reed called papyrus, pasted together side by side to form a roll on which the text was written in a series of columns. The more convenient codex-book to which we are accustomed, together with the smoother parchment (vellum) sheet, only appeared many centuries later. The reader of a papyrus roll was given very little help: there were no regular punctuation marks, headings and paragraphs were erratic even in literary texts, individual words were normally not separated (Plate 1c). Each copy had to be written out by hand, and we must assume that few copies of any book were in existence at any given time. Bookstalls are mentioned in the late fifth century, but one must think of a very modest trade, with circulation chiefly on a personal, non-commercial basis.

It would therefore be a distortion to overstress the written word. The Greeks preferred to talk and listen: even their architecture is that of a people who loved talk; not only the huge outdoor theatres and assembly-halls but also that most characteristic of all Greek structures, the stoa or roofed colonnaded walk. For every person who read a tragedy there were tens of thousands who knew them from performing in them or from hearing them. This was also true of lyric poetry, normally composed for public performance (frequently by choruses) on ceremonial occasions, whether a wedding or a religious festival or to celebrate a military triumph or victory in the games. It was even true, though to a limited extent, of prose. Herodotus, for example, gave public readings from his *History*. Philosophers taught by discourse and discussion. Plato openly expressed his distrust of reliance on books: they cannot be questioned, and therefore their ideas are closed to correction and further refinement, and besides they weaken the memory (*Phaedrus* 274-8). His teacher Socrates out-Johnsoned Dr Johnson and built his reputation solely on a long lifetime of talk, for he never wrote a line.

Plato himself, for all his doubts, was a prolific and most beautiful writer, and characteristically, most of his works are cast in 'dialogue' form, in which his philosophical ideas are developed through complicated discussions, dramatically presented, in real settings with real people who argue and laugh and become angry, precisely as people do under such circumstances. The only other prose writers of the fourth century whose style can be put on some sort of comparable plane were – again characteristically – orators and teachers of rhetoric, such as Isocrates and Demosthenes, who wrote not only genuine speeches but also political pamphlets disguised as orations. This elevation of oratory to a high literary form is the final outcome of the Greek addiction to the spoken word, an aspect of their life which has always to be kept in mind in any consideration of their literature down to the end of the classical period.

Poetry

The oral quality of literature is probably an important part of the explanation for the very slow development of prose. It is not only a question of the late emergence of prose as *belles lettres* – Xenophon in the fourth century is the first significant name in this category – but of the (to us) curious employment of poetry in political and philosophical writing. Solon is an early example: he expressed his political and ethical ideas in elegiac couplets. Even at the end of the sixth century there was Xenophanes, who left Asia Minor an exile and lived in western Greece, and half a century later still, Empedocles of Acragas and Parmenides of Elea, important pre-Socratic philosophers, who wrote only in poetic form. By their time, other philosophers and the earliest writers on geography and history had given prose a certain standing, but since only brief fragments of their work survive, it is not possible to assess their literary qualities. Herodotus is therefore the first Greek of whom it can be said that he was a great and elegant prose stylist. Even after his time there were never many, Plato and the orators apart, though huge quantities of prose were turned out. Poetry retained its position of dominance until the declining centuries of Greek civilization under Roman rule, when a few prose writers, notably Plutarch and Lucian (born *c.* A.D. 46 and *c.* A.D. 120, respectively), brought the story to a close with a flourish.

Poetry underwent a series of interesting changes, reflecting something of the history of Greek society itself. If the begin-

I. GREEK WRITING

TOP: Clay tablet from Cnossus in Crete, Linear B script, about 1400. CENTRE: Metrical epigrams on marble cenotaph, Athens, soon after 490. BOTTOM: Literary papyrus, early third century A.D.

2. THEATRE AT SEGESTA IN SICILY

3. THEATRE AND TEMPLE OF APOLLO, DELPHI

4. TOP: Rim (more than 3 ft in diameter) and handle of bronze urn, Vix (near Châtillon-sur-Seine), late sixth century. BOTTOM LEFT: Graeco-Scythian gold bracelet, about 300. BOTTOM RIGHT: Polychrome terra-cotta antefix, head of Silenus, Gela (Sicily), before 450

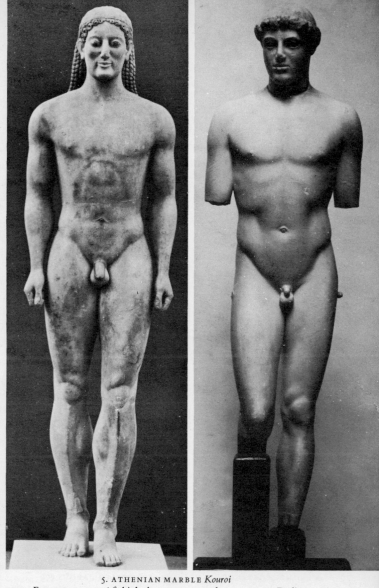

5. ATHENIAN MARBLE *Kouroi*

LEFT: Funerary statue, 6 ft high, between 540 and 520. RIGHT: Dedicatory statue, 2 ft 10 ins. high, not long before 480

6. BRONZE CHARIOTEER, 5 FT 11 INS. HIGH, DELPHI, ABOUT 470

7. BRONZE, 4 FT 3 INS. HIGH, FOUND IN BAY OF MARATHON,
MID FOURTH CENTURY

8. SILVER COINS (*actual size*)
A Athens, tetradrachm, soon after 490. B Syracuse, decadrachm, first minted in
413. C Chalcidian League, tetradrachm, soon after 392. D Amphipolis (coin of
Alexander), tetradrachm, soon after 323

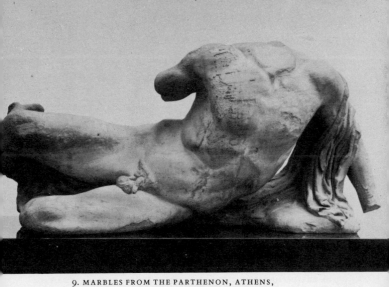

9. MARBLES FROM THE PARTHENON, ATHENS,
THIRD QUARTER OF FIFTH CENTURY

TOP: Two nymphs or goddesses from the east pediment. BOTTOM: River-god from the west pediment

10. ERECHTHEUM ON THE ACROPOLIS, ATHENS, COMPLETED IN 404

II. DETAIL FROM THE ERECHTHEUM

12. MARBLE TOMBSTONE, ATHENS, ABOUT 330

13. METOPE FROM TEMPLE OF HERA, FOCE DEL SELE IN SOUTHERN ITALY, SIXTH CENTURY

Doric: Parthenon

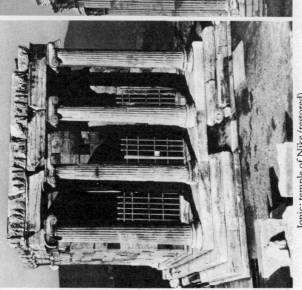

Ionic: temple of Nike (restored)

Corinthian: temple of Olympian Zeus

14–15. THE THREE ARCHITECTURAL ORDERS IN ATHENS

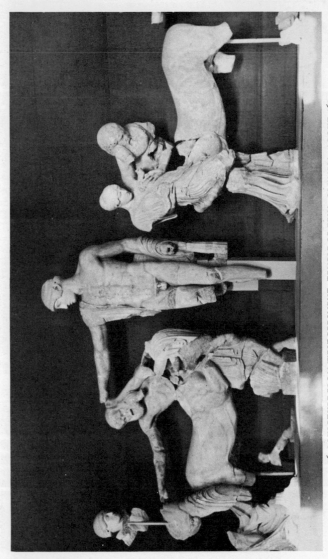

16. SCULPTURE FROM WEST PEDIMENT, TEMPLE OF ZEUS, OLYMPIA, ABOUT 460

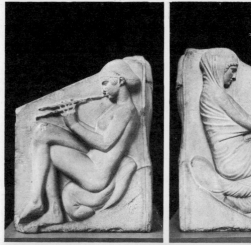

17. SO-CALLED 'LUDOVISI THRONE', MARBLE FROM ITALY,
ABOUT 460

18. POLYCHROME TERRA–COTTA, FOUND IN CAPUA,
PROBABLY THIRD CENTURY

19. DIPYLON AMPHORA, 5 FT HIGH, ATHENS, ABOUT 750

20. ATHENIAN AMPHORA, 16¼ INS. HIGH, BY EXEKIAS, SECOND HALF OF
THE SIXTH CENTURY

21. ATHENIAN AMPHORA, 2 FT HIGH, ABOUT 440

22. CORINTHIAN CUP, 3¾ INS. HIGH, LATE SEVENTH CENTURY

23. BRONZE HEAD, I FT HIGH, CYRENE, PROBABLY
MID FOURTH CENTURY

24. WEST FRONT (RESTORED), GREAT ALTAR OF PERGAMUM, ABOUT 180

ning of the archaic period was marked by the shift from epic to the personal poetry of a man like Archilochus, the transition to the classical period saw another pronounced change. In a sense, of course, poetry is always the personal expression of the individual poet's feelings, ideas and values (though there was a very strong impersonal element in the heroic poetry which culminated in the *Iliad* and *Odyssey*). What is striking about classical Greece is how both the themes and the occasions became those of the community, not of the individual. Poetry like the buccaneering lines of Archilochus, the love poems of Sappho, the drinking-songs of Anacreon virtually ceased to be written. There were exceptions, of course, and minor love poets continued to make a fleeting appearance, but the generalization remains that classical poetry abandoned the purely personal emotions for social, religious and high moral themes.

The transition is most easily perceived in three men who brought the age of lyric poetry to its close: Simonides of Ceos, his nephew Bacchylides and, probably the greatest of them all, the Boeotian poet Pindar, who lived from 518 to about 438. They were all very prolific, and their works include a wide variety of categories, such as hymns, paeans (usually in celebration of military victory), dirges, epigrams, epinician odes (in honour of a victor in the games). The first thing to be noted is that all this poetry was written for specific occasions, usually on commission from a patron. The poets travelled widely and frequently and their work was universal. Each poem was linked with a particular place only because of the occasion or person evoking it, but it was never 'regional' or 'national' as so much modern poetry has always been. Second, religion was part of the fabric itself, so to speak. The paean, for example, was originally a hymn to Apollo, and it never lost that quality, even when it became a hymn to victory and peace. The epinician odes – the best known of all because forty-five of Pindar's poems in this genre have survived in full – started from a religious occasion, the games at a festival, and they celebrated the victor by recounting very complicated myths in a fragmentary or allusive way, tied (no matter how tenuously) to the theme at hand, inter-mixed with moral lessons and maxims and even some political and social comment. In appearance the subject may have been an athlete; in reality it was the community and its gods.

Pindar's second Pythian ode, for example, one of several for Hiero, tyrant of Syracuse from 478 until his death in 467 or 466, opens with obvious appropriateness:*

> Great city, O Syracuse, precinct of Ares
> that haunts the deeps of battle; nurse divine of horses and men
>   that fight in iron,
> from shining Thebes I come, bringing you
> this melody, message of the chariot course that shakes the earth,
> wherein Hiero in success of his horses
> has bound in garlands that gleam far Ortygia. . . .

But before long the poet turns to the singularly unpleasant myth of Ixion, progenitor of the centaurs, who sought to seduce Hera, consort of the king of the gods, and was fittingly punished by being bound to a wheel of fire which revolves eternally. This is a Thessalian myth in origin, having no known connexion with Hiero or Syracuse other than the quite arbitrary didactic one the poet proceeds to give it:*

> It is God that accomplishes all term to hopes,
> God, who overtakes the flying eagle, outpasses the dolphin
> in the sea; who bends under his strength the man with thoughts
>   too high,
> while to others he gives honour that ages not. My necessity
> is to escape the teeth of reproach for excessive blame.
> Standing afar, I saw Archilochus the scold,

* *The Odes of Pindar*, translated by Richmond Lattimore, published by the University of Chicago Press. Copyright 1947 by the University of Chicago.

labouring helpless and fattening on his own cantankerous
hate, naught else; to be rich, with fortune of wisdom also, is the
   highest destiny.

You, in freedom of your heart, can make this plain,
   you, that are prince of garlanded streets in their multitude

and so on. There is much that is obscure in this particular ode
(Pindar is rarely clear-spoken to the modern reader); something, too, of deeply felt personal bitterness, perhaps arising
from the rivalry with Simonides for Hiero's patronage. Nevertheless, this is no longer personal poetry like that of Sappho
and Alcaeus a century or more before. Though Pindar's
poems may still be classified as lyric, in a very restricted
formal sense, even these brief excerpts reveal that psychologically and intellectually the kinship is rather with his Athenian contemporary Aeschylus and the very different art-form
he created.

Tragedy

The lyric poet's individual patron was never wholly lost from
sight, especially if he were a tyrant. It was no accident that
Simonides and Pindar had such close ties to Sicily, or that
Pindar, in particular, was identified in many minds with the
dying world of the traditional aristocracy and with tyranny,
rather than with the new, triumphant classical *polis*. It was
Athens, the democratic city-state *par excellence*, which produced and which was in the strict sense the patron of tragedy,
an art-form soon given the place of honour after Homer over
all other poetry, not only among the Athenians but among
the Greeks generally. Plutarch's story (*Life of Nicias* XXIX)
that some of the Athenians captured in Syracuse in 413 owed
their lives to their ability to recite Euripides from memory

may or may not be fact, but it illustrates admirably the standing tragedy had achieved.

The origins of tragedy are obscure. There is a certain obvious logic about the emergence of lyric poetry: men have always employed song on ceremonial occasions, above all in their relations with their gods, and a lyric poem was, as its name indicates, something sung to the lyre (or, by a later extension, to the flute as well). Often the song, especially if it were choral, accompanied a dance or mime and at times it was considered fitting and necessary that dancers wear masks: for example, to represent the satyrs always associated with Dionysus. Such combinations are so widespread that it is not surprising that in sixth-century Greece there were experiments seeking to bring lyric poetry, which had travelled a long way in its sophistication and formality, into an organic relationship with ancient rituals. Nor is it surprising that Dionysus was the god who was the particular focal point. Like Demeter, the goddess of fertility, he occupied a peculiar place in the pantheon: virtually ignored by Homer and not counted among the Olympians (though a son of Zeus), Dionysus rose to high status in his own way in the official religion of the state while remaining pre-eminently a popular god, the god of wine and revelry, of ecstasies and frenzies and orgiastic rites.

The combination of lyric poetry and Dionysiac ritual provided the pre-history of tragedy, and yet, like most genealogical accounts, this one too explains far less than it pretends. For what emerged was neither ritual dance nor choral celebration of the god nor a straightforward pairing of the two, but something new and different, namely, theatre. The Greeks, or more correctly the Athenians, at this point invented the idea of theatre, as they invented so many other social and cultural institutions which the west then came to take for granted. There is nothing self-evident about the idea of theatre, of plays and players through whom private individuals, lacking priestly or other authority, publicly examined man's fate and commented on it, not by merely singing hymns in praise of the gods nor by ritual drama, as in the re-enactment of the Demeter myth, which seems to have been the culmination of the Eleusinian mysteries (or of the Passion story, to give the most familiar example); but by a poetic play which, despite the many traditional elements, was in its essential qualities a creation of the playwright – in the action of the characters and in the moods, images and comments called up by the long choral passages. The Greeks judged well when they coupled tragedy with epic: in its way this new creation was as bold and revolutionary, with an impact which long outlived the society that produced it.

Tragedy was not ritual drama, then – this point cannot be stressed too strongly – but it retained the closest ties with religion, in the first instance by its integral association with festivals (and therefore, the Greeks being Greeks, by being produced competitively). Most tragedies made their first appearance at the Greater or City Dionysia, held in Athens in the early spring, the most magnificent of the four annual Athenian festivals honouring Dionysus. The first day was given over to a colourful ceremonial procession, climaxed by the sacrifice of a bull and the formal deposition of the statue of the god in the theatre, and then to a contest in dithyrambic odes involving ten choruses, five of men and five of boys, each with fifty members accompanied by flutes. On the second day five comedies were produced. And then came the competition in tragedy extending over three full days, one assigned to each of the competing playwrights, who wrote for the occasion three tragedies (we should call them one-act plays) which might be connected to form a trilogy but need not be, and apparently usually were not, and a fourth play in an entirely different genre, a grotesque 'satyr-play'.

The scale of this whole effort is rather staggering. The active participants numbered no fewer than 1,000 men and boys, who had previously spent much time in rehearsal, and the theatre, if filled, held about 14,000 spectators seated in rising tiers in the open air, looking down on the dancing-floor (called the *orchestra*, merely a cleared circular space) and on the stage behind it, with its simple backdrop and rudimentary stage machinery. The effort was repeated each year, even during the Peloponnesian War, and always with new works. In the course of the fifth century several smaller rural festivals began the practice of staging plays from some earlier City Dionysia, but the first known occasion when an old play was performed a second time at the main festival did not come until 386. Yet writers who could not count on a large reading public were not deterred: year in and year out they wrote new plays in the hope of this single performance – a hope bound to be vain for many, especially those with a lesser reputation, because the rule of one playwright a day for three days was invariant.

The motivating force behind such an output of energy must be sought in the occasion itself, a great communal celebration, solemn and festive at the same time (exceeded in majesty only by the Great Panathenaea, held quadrennially in honour of Athena, the patron goddess of the *polis*). The highest official of the state, the annually elected eponymous archon, presided over the proceedings, and his duties included the selection of the playwrights who were to compete. The far from negligible costs of production were borne in part by the public treasury directly, and partly by assignment to individuals from the wealthiest classes, precisely as the command and some of the financing of the warships were arranged, with the same honorific overtones in the two seemingly incomparable types of activity. And the competition was decided by a panel of five judges, chosen in a complicated way which included the inevitable drawing of lots.

The dramatists were, of course, fully conscious of the occasion, though not, oddly enough, with particular reference to Dionysus, whose myths and functions rarely formed the subject of the plays. It would be easy to quote bits full of high moral sentiment and piety, but the effect would be too puny and essentially misleading. When Aristotle said that of the six constitutive elements of tragedy, 'the most important is the combination of actions, for tragedy is an imitation (*mimesis*) not of men but of action and life' (*Poetics* VI), his analysis points to the need to take each play whole, for the whole is greater than its parts, the action in that sense greater than the music and the poetry and the individual characterizations, essential as each of these elements also was. Only seeing (or reading) a tragedy in one continuous sitting can give the proper effect: the unrelieved tension, the elevated tone and often opaque poetic language, the long, complicated speeches and odes, full of allusions and oracular obscurities, the total concentration on the most fundamental questions of human existence, of man's behaviour and destiny under divine power and authority. It was this total effect which invested tragedy with its highest religious quality, made more concrete and vivid by direct reference to oracles, prophecies and gods; by the use of myth as the normal source of the story itself; by the many hymn-like passages of choral singing; by the masks and costumes and dances to which the Greeks were accustomed in their rites.

Of the many remarkable features of Greek tragedy, none is so astonishing as the unchallenged monopoly which the Athenians maintained. The sixth-century experiments seem to have begun in Corinth and Sicyon in the Peloponnese, but once the Athenians took an interest (according to tradition the credit goes to Thespis in the time of Peisistratus) further progress was entirely in their hands. Until well in the fourth century tragedies were performed regularly only in Athens, and all the plays were apparently written in the first instance for the Athenian competitions. Non-Athenian playwrights were free to submit and sometimes they even carried off the first prize, yet not one case has survived in the records of such a man writing a tragedy for home consumption. Aeschylus twice went to Sicily, and that is significant chiefly because it was so exceptional in his day: in telling about the Athenian prisoners Plutarch explained that the Sicilian Greeks, enamoured of Euripides, were dependent on the snatches they picked up from travellers and learned by heart.

Aeschylus, Sophocles and Euripides together spanned the fifth century. Between them they wrote approximately 300 plays, thirty-two of which survive. We do not possess a single play by any of the other 150-odd writers of tragedy whose names are known, some of them men with a once considerable reputation. There is reason to believe that the process of selection through the ages was not a bad one. From the middle of the fourth century repetition of old plays became habitual, as did the presentation of the same old plays in many parts of Hellas. Travelling companies of 'Dionysiac artists' now became a feature of Greek cultural life, and the actors, Aristotle complained in the *Rhetoric* (III 1, 4), 'now count for more than the poets'. He might have said that the buildings, too, were becoming more important: the fifth-century Theatre of Dionysus was still a crude affair, to be transformed in the fourth century into a splendid stone amphitheatre and to be paralleled in Delphi, Epidaurus and elsewhere (Plates 2 and 3). After the Peloponnesian War, in sum, though tragedy continued as a popular art for a long time, it rapidly became a secondary, derivative art, living on the old masters rather than on vital new creation.

Evidently fifth-century Athens somehow provided the atmosphere in which this art could flourish. It would be foolhardy to make the further suggestion that the link between tragedy and democracy was a simple, direct one. Political allusions are not infrequent in the plays, and a few, like Aeschylus' *Persians*, written less than ten years after the battle of Salamis, abandoned the realm of myth for a contemporary setting. There was nothing inconsistent or inappropriate in this: the Greater Dionysia was a community celebration, religion was a *polis* affair, and when the playwrights touched on politics it was the moral implications they projected, not practical politics. They were neither pamphleteers nor political theorists or propagandists (unless one wishes to speak of propaganda for morality and in a general sense for justice). Indeed, their private political views remain very elusive (one is reminded of Shakespeare).

If there is a tie with the democratic atmosphere of fifth-century Athens it must be sought on another level – in the way the dramatists were encouraged, so to speak, to explore the human soul and in the tolerance shown in circumstances in which that particular quality is not what one might have expected. Festival conditions imposed definite limits on the artists, in the employment of actors and chorus, in their choice of themes, even in the structure of the plays and in their poetic language and metre. Aeschylus introduced a second actor, perhaps the decisive technical step in actually creating the art-form itself; then Sophocles added a third, and that was the end of that development. The role of the chorus was gradually but persistently minimized, until Euripides in many of his plays reduced it to little more than a musical interlude. With Euripides one often has the feeling that, if he could, he would have burst through the established frame altogether. He could not and still remain an Attic tragedian, but he, like his predecessors, could probe with astonishing latitude and freedom into the traditional myths and beliefs, and into fresh problems society was throwing up, such as the new Socratic emphasis on reason, or the humanity of slaves, or the responsibilities and corruption of power. They did so annually under the auspices of the state and Dionysus, before the largest gatherings of men, women and children (and even slaves) ever assembled in Athens. Seats of honour were among the highest prizes the state could bestow, sought after by distinguished foreigners and natives alike. It is, of course, impossible to recapture the feelings of these vast audiences, many of whom regularly sat through three long days of difficult and complex poetic drama. But one can register the phenomenon and ponder its implications.

Comedy

The publication in 1958 of a papyrus written in the third century A.D. (Plate 1c) made available the text of the *Dyskolos* or *Misanthrope*, an early and inferior play by the Athenian poet Menander (born in 342 or 341). Previously the only Greek comedies we possessed in full were eleven by another and greater Athenian, Aristophanes (born about 450). Like tragedy, classical comedy was an Athenian monopoly, and the plays were produced competitively at Dionysiac festivals. But there the parallels cease. In the broad sense of the word, some form of comedy was probably ubiquitous in the Greek world. What the Athenians developed and made their own was the full-scale poetic play, with few actors and a chorus. In the fifth century, in so-called 'Old Comedy', the players wore exaggerated and grotesque costumes, engaged in quantities of horse-play, were exuberant and raucous and flagrantly obscene, and at moments turned lyrical and serious. Superficially there were more vestiges of ritual, of processions and masques and feasting, in comedy than in tragedy – but only on the surface: for not only was comedy in no proper sense ritual drama, it was fundamentally not religious in any sense. No Greek was likely to talk for many minutes without some reference to the gods and myths, and that was true of comedy as well. But rarely was religion its theme, even in a minor key, despite the festival background.

The comic poets dealt chiefly in the contemporary scene in all its rich variety, its politics, customs and habits, fads and fashions, aspirations, vices, its newfangled ideas and dead traditions, its generals and soldiers, peasants and philosophers and fancy boys and slaves. Free from the canonical trammels of the tragic poets – and it was the rarest exception for a man to try his hand at both comedy and tragedy – the comic playwrights employed every stylistic device they could dream up to pour a stream of ridicule and abuse on both personalities and ideas, and not even the gods escaped their appetite for victims. Sometimes the targets were disguised, though rarely enough to fool any reasonably informed spectator, but often they were called by their right names, like Socrates in the *Clouds*, for example, or Euripides in the *Acharnians*, *Frogs* and *Thesmophorazusae*.

We can judge Old Comedy only from Aristophanes, and that is not easy to do in depth. His wit and inventiveness were boundless, as was the savagery of his invective, and he possessed a penetrating mind. He was also capable of poetry of great beauty and earnestness. What often escapes us, unfortunately, is the dividing-line between the two aspects. When was a joke only a joke and not a wounding blow, and how serious – with what aim in mind – were the serious passages? Of his first ten plays, all produced during the first half of the Peloponnesian War, seven were political in subject, and they were filled with barbs thrown at the popular leaders, beginning with Pericles, at institutions like the jury-courts and at the war itself. They were rough jokes, far more so than would be tolerated in the modern music-hall revue. Yet it does not necessarily follow, in a simple logical step, that Aristophanes was therefore against the Athenian democracy and against the war with Sparta; or that his picture of the demagogues, the populace and the jury-courts is balanced and accurate, or was intended to be. For one thing, passages can be quoted from the surviving plays on both sides of many of the issues. For another, there is the fact that Aristophanes won four first prizes, three second and one third during his career, apparently the most successful record in Old Comedy; and this suggests that his audiences, enough of whom were surely not anti-democratic and anti-war, did not look upon him as the outspoken political enemy he is often made out to be by modern students. On the other hand, the alternative extreme, that it was all good clean fun, with no offence intended or taken, reduces the whole affair to froth, to superficial laughter which left nothing behind. Plato, at least, took a more serious view when he had Socrates say in defending himself in court in the year 399 (*Apology* 18): 'The accusers I really fear are the men who spread false rumours about my work, that I specialize, for example, in making the worse argument appear the better. These men I cannot cross-examine. I neither know their names nor can say who they are, unless one happens to be a comic poet.' The reference to Aristophanes is then made explicit, and Plato's testimony to the lasting impact of the *Clouds* cannot be dismissed out of hand.

Probably the line can no longer be drawn with confidence, but on any view the implications are clear enough. Where else does one find annual public festivals, religious ones at that, which are given over to continuous lampooning of the most cherished institutions, and more remarkable still, to anti-war jokes and speeches in the midst of a great and critical war – all a state activity, from the initial choice of the plays to the final crowning of the victorious playwright? And all done with such a flair and such a critical sense that many of the jokes and scenes are still uproarious more than two thousand years later? Nor was Aristophanes a unique figure. Although he had the greatest success in winning prizes, writers like Cratinus and Eupolis were not far behind. Some apparently took a less bilious view of Athenian politics and politicians, but on the whole Old Comedy was all of a piece, a general phenomenon which lasted for about half a century. Perhaps nothing else reflects certain qualities of fifth-century Athens so exactly, its wide freedoms, its self-confidence, its vitality and exuberance, and the capacity of the *demos* to laugh at itself.

The end of the Peloponnesian War also saw the end of this kind of comedy. Fourth-century comedy was from the beginning, even in the late plays of Aristophanes, quieter in tone, less pungent and hard-hitting, on the whole less immediate in its social and political content. By the middle of the century it had become an altogether different art-form (thus following a different course from tragedy, which froze and became sterile). 'New Comedy', reaching its climax in Menander, abandoned current affairs, current political ideas and broad social issues altogether. It became a comedy of manners, respectable, safe, scarcely as bawdy as Restoration comedy in England, restricted to fictitious characters and monotonous conventionalized plots accurately summed up in the title of the Shakespearean play, directly descended from New Comedy – a comedy of errors. The interest was now narrowed to the portrayal of stock characters, to obvious moralizing around the virtue-triumphant motif and to the poet's skill in turning a phrase or resolving a situation. Aristophanic plots centred round the efforts, half-serious, half-zany, of a free individual, acting on his own initiative, to meet a major public crisis or abate some supposedly great evil, such as the Peloponnesian War, the pernicious teachings of the Sophists, the bad poetry of Euripides and his attitude to women; Menander's on clever and usually crooked tricks to rescue a girl from a pimp or bring together two lovers, private troubles which free men could not cope with, only slaves.

Matters of taste may be beyond discussion, but it is difficult to avoid the conclusion that New Comedy was appropriate to the final days of Athenian independence, when the *polis* was struggling to survive, and even more to the politically dead Athens of the half-century after Alexander the Great. And it retained its popularity over Old Comedy for a long time, with the Romans as well, among whom it became widely known and loved in Latin adaptations and imitations by Plautus and Terence (whose lives spanned the century 250–150). One cannot imagine the Rome of the Carthaginian Wars countenancing, let alone enjoying, an Aristophanic character like Dicaeopolis in the *Acharnians* sitting on the Pnyx and saying: 'I have come here to shout, interrupt, and hurl abuse every time a speaker talks about anything but peace.'

Prose

A steadily increasing volume of prose writing was technical in nature: philosophy, law and politics, science and technology, all had their literatures. They need to be noticed, however, solely for their subject-matter, not (with rare exceptions) as art. Only history stands apart, and later oratory. For a long time the Greeks' interest in the past was satisfied by their stock of myths and legends, which were believed to be true; even sceptics like the philosopher Xenophanes, who challenged the morality taught by the tales and their crude supernaturalism, never doubted the existence of Agamemnon, king of Mycenae, or of Oedipus of Thebes, Greeks not too different from themselves who lived in an undated 'once upon a time' in which they ruled, fought and begat. The interest was not historical in the sense of an inquiry into the facts of the

Trojan War or of any other occurrence or period, but something quite different. Hellenic or regional consciousness and pride, the sanction for power, the meaning of cult practices, community solidarity – that was what one sought to warrant or reinforce from the past, and such ends were admirably served by the old tales, with revisions when demanded by new historical developments, political and social changes – all made easy by the great range and quantity of the available myths and by the imprecision inevitable in oral transmission.

A new turn came in Asia Minor towards the end of the sixth century, stimulated by special local conditions. There the Greeks were subjected to the overlordship of barbarian kingdoms, first Lydia and then Persia, and they naturally developed a curiosity about these people which could not be satisfied by Greek myths about Greeks. Books appeared to meet the demand, giving all kinds of information (and as often, misinformation), geographical, descriptive of social and religious customs, and, in a fragmentary way, historical. The number of these writers, known as logographers, should not be exaggerated, nor the quality of their work, but at the same time the novelty and originality of the enterprise is notable. Nothing like it had ever been attempted before, neither among the Greeks nor among the other nations they knew, first in the breach of ethnocentrism and then in the destructive backlash on their own traditions. 'What I write here', said Hecataeus of Miletus, who incidentally played a leading part in the Ionian revolt against Persia, 'is the account I believe to be true. For the stories the Greeks tell are many, and in my opinion ridiculous.' Hecataeus was here speaking about Greek history, not barbarian, and those two simple sentences are the first tentative step from myth to historical inquiry.

Then came a great leap, the work of a single man, another native of Asia Minor. Herodotus of Halicarnassus had the idea of extending the scope of logography to take in a much wider area, including the Scythians and Egyptians, for example, along with the Lydians and Persians; and the idea, too, of trying to control the mass of accumulated data (some of it now in writing, the remainder still available only orally) by personal investigations on the spot through a series of quick visits to all the places, by a rational analysis of the information he assembled and by the use of the royal annals of Assyria, Persia and Egypt to help establish an exact chronology, at least for the previous 100 or 150 years. This would have been achievement enough, but eventually he went still further. A political refugee from Halicarnassus, Herodotus lived in Samos and then in Athens. There apparently, under the impact of Periclean Athens at its height, he made his most radical decision, namely, that he would write the history of the Persian Wars. The daring of this undertaking is astonishing. Nearly a generation had gone by since the wars had ended. Scarcely any documentation was available in writing. Yet Herodotus set about reconstructing the story in all its detail, by drawing on the memory of survivors and of men in the next generation who remembered the tales they had been told.

The book Herodotus finally produced was a complicated one, retaining in its first half much of the original logography, but all of it held together by the great central theme of the struggle between Greeks and Persians. Beyond a doubt he had earned the title of 'Father of History'. He was a great artist as well, which cannot be said of many of his successors. Nor, for that matter, were they great historians either. Herodotus met with a very mixed reception from the beginning. Father of History – Father of Lies: that cry was never stilled in antiquity, and even today Herodotus is often badly misjudged as if he were no more than a story-teller with a charming style and boundless credulity.

One man who knew better was the Athenian Thucydides. He saw what Herodotus was really trying to do, namely, to uncover the mainsprings of human behaviour by a systematic account of the causes and conduct of a great war, not as the poets did it with their imaginative freedom, nor abstractly as the philosophers might discourse about men and society, but concretely, accurately and with due attention to sequences and connexions. And he thought he could do it better, by more intense concentration on factual accuracy, by absolute austerity in eliminating 'romance' from the account, by narrowing the focus to war and politics, by closer definition of 'causes', by excluding the supernatural from the picture and leaving the stage wholly to his one subject, man. Thucydides wrote the history of the Peloponnesian War, in which he was himself a participant in the early stages (giving him an enormous advantage over Herodotus), and he devoted his life to his *History* with remarkable single-mindedness. Those portions of the book which are most general, and, in a sense, most philosophical, are written with great power and brilliance. The narrative proper is uneven, rising to heights in the Sicilian expedition but often drifting into a boring succession of unimportant and uninteresting details. The style is sometimes crabbed, especially in the speeches, and rarely elegant. Yet reading and re-reading Thucydides is always a memorable experience because he approached his great theme with the utmost seriousness of purpose and with moral fervour, not satisfied merely to describe and narrate but constantly seeking, at the same time, what is most permanent and universal in man and politics, firm in the conviction that human nature is immutable and supremely important, its study worth the whole of a man's life.

Thereafter history, though it grew in popularity and many men tried their hand at it, went into a permanent decline. Nothing else in the Greek achievement was so abortive: two men of genius stood at the beginning, to be followed by many centuries of quantity without quality, in which neither

Herodotus nor Thucydides served as a model, let alone as initiators whose methods and conceptions required refinement and modification. Serious study of psychology and morality passed to the philosophers; history became either pedestrian fact-finding or a vehicle for political propaganda and emotional appeal; a writer's success was measured by his rhetoric and pathos, his entertainment value, rather than by truth and understanding. Only occasionally does someone rear himself out of the ruck and show something of the earnestness or vision of the two fifth-century giants. The best of them among the survivors, Polybius writing in the second century B.C. and Dio Cassius early in the third century A.D., were actually historians of Rome rather than of Greece. And a word should be spared for Diodorus the Sicilian who compiled a world history from the beginning of time to Caesar's Gallic Wars (of which he was a young contemporary). His vast work was appropriately called a *Library of Universal History*; Diodorus lacked the capacity to do much more than cut and paste, or even to do that with sufficient skill, but he did have a vision, rare in his time, of a universal humanity. All these men are indispensable for the information they provide; none of them merits study as a literary figure or even as an exponent of the art of history.

In a formal sense, history had quickly fallen victim to the great curse of post-fifth-century Greek culture – rhetoric. The emergence of oratory as an art-form in itself was but one example of a pervasive evil. Another was manifest in education; Isocrates triumphed over Plato and rhetoric was elevated above philosophy in the curriculum of the higher schools which became a feature of Hellenistic and Roman Greece. The servant had become master: the manner in which an idea was expressed became more important than the idea itself. This was already too evident in the fourth century; it became the rule in the Hellenistic age.

Relatively little of Hellenistic *belles lettres* survives, but there is no reason to believe that what has been lost would seriously alter the picture. Such creative vitality as that age had was poured into philosophy and science. There is something cold, lifeless and essentially rhetorical and empty about even the best of its literature, whether the hymns of Callimachus or the pastoral idylls of Theocritus or the love epigrams preserved in the *Greek Anthology*, though the construction is subtle, the phrasing pretty. The shorter poems return to the private concerns of archaic literature, as do the late prose romances, stories of love and adventure like *Daphnis and Chloe*. But with what a difference: passion has been reduced to sentimentality, men and women to stock figures even more lifeless than those of New Comedy, their world to a child's fairyland. Archilochus and Sappho grasped reality by the throat, Meleager and Longus fled from it to eroticism and clever word-pictures. Only the very rare exception broke the monotony: Plutarch, a brilliant, erudite and widely ranging essayist and biographer, who succeeded in recapturing something of the zest and depth of the long-dead classical civilization, despite the heavy drag of his own time and despite a cavalier indifference to what we (or Thucydides) should call historical truth. Or Lucian, the most astonishing sport (in the biologist's sense) of them all: a professional rhetorician earning at least some of his living by giving public declamations, who in his finest writings mocked at the cant and hypocrisy of his day, especially in religion and popular philosophy, in a manner and a language not unworthy of Aristophanes. It is hardly surprising that he was not much thought of in the bleak, autocratic age of the Antonine emperors; his current neglect is another matter.

The bookish quality unmistakable in all these writers was appropriate to an age whose major contribution to literature lay in scholarship. Led by the Library and Museum founded in Alexandria by Ptolemy I, one of Alexander's generals who established the Macedonian dynasty in Egypt, Hellenistic scholars tried to assemble the whole corpus of Greek literature, catalogued it, established reasonably accurate texts, elaborated the rules of grammar and composition and performed many other comparable services. Valuable as this work was, it represented another kind of interest from the literary activity which had been the hallmark of Hellas from Homer's time on.

CHAPTER 6

SCIENCE, PHILOSOPHY AND
POPULAR MORALS

GREEK religion, when we can first read about it – in the *Iliad* and *Odyssey* and Hesiod's *Theogony* – already had a long history behind it. Not so Greek philosophy: the kind of inquiry into the nature of the universe which was initiated by the Ionian philosophers of Miletus at the beginning of the sixth century was completely original. Thereafter philosophy was vigorously pursued by the Greeks down to the end of the ancient world, and no one period or region held a monopoly. It ranged widely, encompassing both theology and science, and it succeeded in escaping the perils of scholasticism, of becoming fixed in some traditional mould and degenerating into a sterile restatement or over-refinement of accepted authority. Aristotle was that kind of authority in the Middle Ages, for whom he was 'the philosopher'; but not in antiquity, which allowed no man that claim although it recognized in Homer 'the poet'.

What is the world? What is man? These were not new questions. But previously the answers were mythical; they were stories, often with a genealogical quality or flavour. Earth gave birth to the sky. Zeus, Poseidon and Hades were three brothers who overthrew the Titans and divided the universe among themselves into three realms. Man was *created*. Such mythical answers are world-wide in one form or another, and their quality as explanation is always essentially the same. Myth is specific and concrete, explaining both natural and human phenomena by reference to particular supernatural events or actions, in themselves unaccountable. The Ionian revolution was simply this, that Thales and his successors asked generalized questions and proposed general, rational, 'impersonal' answers. To be sure, they began by naïve speculation, and such suggestions as, 'The earth stays in place through floating like a log', do not get us very far. Nevertheless, it is impossible to over-estimate the boldness of the effort itself, or the significance for the future of intellectual endeavour.

The notion that the earth floats on water was familiar in several Near-Eastern versions, and Thales undoubtedly took it from there. He was, however, not merely borrowing a myth to fill out a gap in the traditional Greek stock, but was seeking something new and different, something unmythical, though he became too shadowy and legendary a figure to permit us to recover his ideas with any precision or confidence. The Greek tradition about him was quite firm: he was the first of the 'physicists' – *physis* is the Greek word for 'nature' – and that label is a clear direction-sign. In the next generation another Milesian, Anaximenes, suggested, in Aristotle's words (*Metaphysics*, I 3), that air is 'the material principle above the other simple bodies', a generalization which he justified on the argument that, by rarefaction or condensation, air can alter its appearance without undergoing a change in its nature. This may not be right, but the attempt to find intelligible principles and coherence beneath the manifold appearances in the cosmos is to replace myth by philosophy. 'Philosophers from Thales onward', Bertrand Russell once wrote, 'have tried to understand the world.' Understanding begins when the right questions are posed and the need for (and possibility of) generalization is perceived; on both scores it is correct to start the history of philosophy with Thales.

Nor can there be much doubt that these men knew that they were on to something exciting. That feeling shines through the scraps of their writing which have been preserved (garbled as they often are), if not in the actual wording at least in their boldness and range, indeed in their exuberant excesses and dogmatism. A third Milesian, Anaximander, according to the not very reliable tradition a pupil of Thales and teacher of Anaximenes, is reported to have said that 'in the beginning man was born from creatures of a different kind; because other creatures are soon self-supporting, but man alone needs prolonged nursing. For this reason he would not have survived if this had been his original form'. That is very acute, but then he suggested that the progenitors of the human species were 'either fish or creatures very like fish; in these men grew, in the form of embryos retained within until puberty; then at last the fish-like creatures burst and men and women who were already able to nourish themselves stepped forth'.*

Not much later in the sixth century a school of Greek philosophy began to flourish in Italy. Its first great name was Pythagoras, an exile from Samos who settled in Croton, where he and his disciples not only made the discoveries which gave Pythagoras legendary fame in the history of mathematics but also turned their attention to the soul and elaborated a doctrine of transmigration and reincarnation. This was one of the ways by which philosophy returned from its earliest and largely exclusive concern with the cosmos and the nature of being generally (which soon led to a consideration of the nature of knowledge and problems of logic) to man himself and to man's relation with the eternal. The Pythagoreans formed a sacred community, requiring secrecy among the initiates, with a mystical doctrine that somehow – though all this is now hopelessly obscure – drew them into the complicated politics of the Greek cities in Italy, where they became centres of faction and revolution.

Once philosophy extended its scope from cosmology to ethics and politics, it never lost this intense involvement in the actual life of its age already to be seen among the Pytha-

* Translated in G. S. Kirk and J. E. Raven, *The Presocratic Philosophers* (Cambridge, 1962), p. 141.

goreans, though not in equal measure or in the same directions among all philosophers or all philosophical schools. Plato was impregnated with Pythagorean mysticism, but not Aristotle. Both had an abiding interest in politics, whereas a philosopher like Diogenes the Cynic dismissed science, politics and organized religion together as vanities – and worse. Yet the generalization stands that Greek philosophy was engaged, often in ways quite alien to modern conceptions.

Science

A Greek of, say, the late fourth century had an adequate vocabulary with which to describe a man as an architect, mathematician, meteorologist, physician or botanist, but he would not have been able to translate the peculiarly narrow English word 'scientist' except by saying 'philosopher' (or, what amounted to the same thing, 'physicist'). If he knew his Aristotle he would have had a precise word for 'science', *episteme*, and a clear conception of what distinguished science from other forms of mental activity: a scientist knows not only that something is so, which is what experience reveals, but why it is so; he has acquired by reason 'knowledge of causes and first principles' (*Metaphysics*, I 1). That is wisdom, *sophia*, hence its possessor is a philosopher, a lover of wisdom. The philosopher and the scientist were identical in their interests and objectives, more often than not in their persons as well. In the early period this personal identity was complete, but with increasing knowledge, specialists appeared and a certain divergence of interest. There were philosophers like Socrates who dismissed science (in our sense) as an inferior concern; on the other hand there were men of medicine or astronomy who showed little interest in the metaphysical and epistemological implications of their studies or in ethics or aesthetics. But no real breach ever occurred: the philosopher-scientist remained the recognized type, and a Greek would not have been able to comprehend such a statement as Whitehead's in *Science and the Modern World*:

Science has never shaken off the impress of its origin in the historical revolt of the later Renaissance. It has remained predominantly an anti-rationalistic movement, based upon naïve faith. . . . Science repudiates philosophy. In other words, it has never cared to justify its faith or to explain its meanings. . . .

The breach which opened in antiquity was located along a quite different line. By the end of the archaic period the Greeks had accumulated a very considerable body of empirical knowledge in agronomy, human anatomy and physiology, engineering, metallurgy, mineralogy, astronomy and navigation. We know next to nothing about the men who made the observations and transmitted the information, nor about the ways in which they worked, presumably because they were craftsmen who in their age-old manner learned and taught by doing, not by reading and writing. The practical consequences, however, are widely attested – in the pottery, the buildings, the sculptures, the range and variety of food products, the developments in navigation – and though much was inherited from older civilizations, much was surely new with the Greeks. But increasingly there was visible a block to further progress, becoming more and more severe as time went on, which can be expressed, somewhat crudely and with full allowance for exceptions, as the growing divorce between theory and practice, between, in modern terminology, pure and applied science. Knowledge was good, wisdom the highest good, but its aim was to know, not to do; to understand man and nature in a contemplative way, rather than to conquer or change nature, to increase efficiency or improve production.

It was Plato who took the most extreme position. For him the whole world of experience, being impermanent, imperfect, 'unreal', could never be the subject of true knowledge, which must be directed to the Ideas or Forms which were eternal and real. He was therefore fundamentally antagonistic to all science that was not reducible to mathematics, and particularly, geometry. Plutarch relates that he criticized those mathematicians who tackled the problem of the duplication of the cube by making physical models, for 'the good of geometry is thereby lost and destroyed, as it is brought back to the things of sense instead of being directed upward and grasping at eternal and incorporeal things' (*Convivial Questions*, 718F). That story may or may not be true, but there is no questioning what Plato himself wrote in the *Republic* (530B) about 'gaping upwards' to study the heavens: 'If we mean to turn the soul's native intelligence to its proper use by a genuine study of astronomy, we shall proceed, as we do in geometry, by means of problems, and leave the starry heavens alone.'*

Scarcely anyone ever took that advice literally, not even Plato himself. Little as we know about the Pythagoreans, we may safely assert that they did not discover the mathematical relationships between musical tones by mere contemplation or mystical revelation, any more than Plato got his vast and very precise knowledge of the laws of Athens and Crete from Apollo, whose son he became in the legends. Not long before Plato's birth there was established on the island of Cos the Hippocratic school of medicine, a most remarkable research organization which in the half century from 440 to 390 performed prodigies of systematic observation and rigorously rational analysis, set down in such works as the first book of *Epidemics* or the little treatise on the 'sacred disease' (epilepsy). In the next century Aristotle and his students reached perhaps

* Translated by F. M. Cornford (Oxford, 1941).

even greater heights in their work in biology, petrology and physiological psychology. Astronomers and mathematical geographers went on gaping upwards and refining their instruments as well as their mathematics, and their achievement, summed up in the great book, usually known by the title the Arabs later gave it, the *Almagest*, of Claudius Ptolemy, an Alexandrian of the second century A.D. (when Ptolemy had long ceased to be a royal name), remained authoritative until it was disrupted by the discoveries of Kepler and Galileo. Military engineers, especially those under the patronage of Philip and Alexander and then of the first Macedonian rulers of Egypt, invented siege weapons and other devices by systematic research into both materials and physical processes. Advances went on in empirical physics until Hero of Alexandria, in his *Pneumatics*, probably written in the first century A.D., was able to describe nine different mechanical devices powered by heated air or steam.

On the mathematical and scientific side, in sum, the process of rational inquiry initiated by the first Ionian cosmologists had travelled a very long way. The Hippocratic practice of auscultation of the heart, Euclid's *Elements*, Archimedes' discovery of specific gravity, the treatise on conic sections by his younger contemporary Apollonius of Perga, Eratosthenes' estimate of the diameter of the earth to within a few hundred miles of the correct figure, Hipparchus's calculation of the precession of the equinoxes, Hero's steam-operated toys – such achievements, to single out a few highlights, were not to be equalled in Europe for another 1,500 years.

Once one looks at the dates, however, the question of blockage becomes obvious and acute. Hipparchus died before the end of the second century B.C., and it was essentially his astronomy that Ptolemy fixed in the *Almagest*. Ptolemy's *Geography*, which gained equally authoritative status, is distorted throughout, at times grossly so; first, because he rejected the calculations made by Eratosthenes (who died in 194) for the later and far less accurate estimates of Poseidonius; second, because his positions, though given in exact terms of latitude and longitude, were in fact rarely based on astronomical calculations (which he knew to be the only reliable procedure). From 375 at the latest, ancient medicine could only struggle to maintain the level to which the Hippocratics had brought it, so that Galen of Pergamum, its last great ancient figure, was no farther ahead more than five hundred years later, and much writing (as well as practice) had fallen well behind. By about 250 military technology reached an impasse from which it never extricated itself. Siege instruments for both offence and defence – the chief task set the engineers – balanced each other so effectively that both sides simply wasted considerable resources in building them.

What emerges is that astronomy, theoretical physics and mathematics prospered long after the applied sciences, and that all science came to a virtual standstill when the ancient world still had many centuries of life ahead. In some respects this is a familiar enough phenomenon in the history of science, *a priori* assumptions or mere habits of mind holding up progress until someone thinks to re-examine them. Perhaps such a purely intellectual explanation will suffice for the low level of Greek interest in algebra, the laws of probability or the laws of terrestrial motion. But it surely will not explain the regressions – not just the standing still – or the totality of the blockage, in all branches of science. On the practical side, some ideas outran the technical capacity of the society, as today, and that explains why Hero could do no more with his knowledge of pneumatics than produce ingenious toys. And again the explanation is insufficient: no one even tried to overcome the technical obstacles; but then, no one thought of the far simpler idea of transferring the well-known principle of the sailing-boat to other, equally essential uses by constructing a wind-mill.

All this stands out most clearly in the school of Aristotle. Although his debt to Plato is visible throughout his work, Aristotle rejected his master's Forms for a thoroughgoing empiricism: the world of experience is what one needs to understand and therefore that is what one starts with – all experience, for he had an intellectual energy and curiosity that have never been surpassed and rarely been approached. 'Those whom indulgence in long discussions has rendered unobservant of facts, are too ready to dogmatize from few observations' (*De generatione et corruptione*, 3169a). His great-est concentration was on biology; at least that subject occupies nearly one-third of the Aristotelian corpus, and the researches were continued by Theophrastus, who succeeded him at the head of the Lyceum, as the school he founded in Athens in or soon after 335 came to be known. Theophrastus was followed by Strato, whose interests lay on the physical rather than the biological side. By the time Strato died (not later than 268) Greek science, it is said, had been brought to the threshold of modernity, most notably in the growing appreciation of ex-perimentalism. But though science lingered on the threshold for perhaps three centuries – there are direct quotations from Strato in Hero's *Pneumatics* – it failed to cross over and even-tually it turned away altogether.

What was missing was an intangible factor, a Baconian spirit which regularly and persistently turns speculation into empirical research, empirical research into practical applica-tion. Aristotle and Theophrastus had vast knowledge of ani-mal breeding and plant yields, but neither they nor their readers drew the conclusions which would lead to selective breeding in agriculture and sheep-farming. Their interest was satisfied when they understood purpose, function, final causes in nature. Or to take another kind of example: Leucippus and

Democritus in the second half of the fifth century propounded an atomic theory of matter which was later adopted by Epicurus and which found its best-known written expression in a long Latin poem, *On the Nature of Things*, by Lucretius (first century B.C.). But atomism, though discussed for centuries, never entered the realm of science in antiquity. Unlike modern atomic theory, the Greek speculations about atoms neither came into being as an attempt to offer a better explanation of empirical observations nor led to more advanced scientific investigation along new lines.

Were this only a matter of individual psychology, sooner or later a break would probably have come. But beneath there lay something much deeper: Greek science and philosophy were 'aristocratic' in the sense that they developed among the leisured classes, for whom the only acceptable practical pursuits were war and statecraft, poetry and oratory. When Aristotle concerned himself with practical arts it was precisely these (except for war) which he studied and wrote about, in his customary, empirical, systematic way. Yet even they belonged to a lower order of study, for a *techne*, conventionally translated 'art' in the sense which includes 'craft' (and ignoring Aristotle's further distinction between making and doing), cannot be a science, an *episteme*. A *techne* is 'a rational quality concerned with making' and 'the term *sophia* is employed in the arts to denote those men who are the most perfect masters of their art; for instance, it is applied to Pheidias as a sculptor and Polycleitus as a statuary. In this use, then, *sophia* merely means artistic excellence' (*Ethics* VI 4–7).* There is no contempt here for the craftsmen, the makers and doers, as there no doubt was among the upper classes generally. Nor is there in Plato, even though in his ideal Republic the ruling-class of philosophers were to be barred from all practical arts other than governing, and were to be trained for many years on a

* Translated by H. Rackham in the Loeb Classical Library.

rigid and restricted diet of mathematics, music (that is, harmonics) and philosophy. The Platonic dialogues are filled with arguments drawn from the analogy of the craftsman, always with genuine respect, as in Aristotle, for vocational skill and excellence. But – and this is the crucial point – there was a hierarchy of values according to which art is an inferior activity, the best pilot or physician inferior in worth to the philosopher, because no matter how necessary and useful his art, it serves a lower-ranking good.

In one form or another, such judgements are common, indeed commonplace, in Greek writing in an unbroken line from at least the fifth century on. Some historians argue that one should not place undue stress on them because they reflect only a small section of the population and were not typical of the general attitude of the Greeks, most of whom were working farmers and craftsmen. The first flaw in this argument is that it was the minority alone who mattered in the history of Greek thought, including scientific thought. They produced the intellectuals who devoted themselves to science and philosophy, and the effect of the generally accepted value-system was to channel their efforts away from practical concerns (other than politics) to the abstractions of mathematics and metaphysics. Not even the most promising of the exceptions, the empiricism of the Aristotelians, could hold out for very long, brilliant as their achievements were.

Besides, there is no evidence (and no good reason to expect any) that the little man had any relevant counter-values to offer. Workmanship of the finest quality was abundant. Good craftsmen were constantly improving their knowledge of materials and processes, in ways which left no trace in the written records. Nevertheless, the fact remains that the basic Greek technology was fixed early in the archaic period, both in agriculture and in manufacture, and that there were few major break-throughs thereafter. The list of Greek inventions is a very short one indeed. Apparently the society as a whole lacked the mentality and the motivation to strive systematically for greater efficiency and greater productivity. Not even so practical a man as Vitruvius, not a philosopher but a working engineer and architect, shows the slightest awareness of the possibilities of technological progress; and his *De Architectura*, written in Latin probably at the very beginning of the Christian era, more or less contemporary with Hero, summed up the most advanced Greek technical knowledge as it had come down the centuries both in books and in actual practice.

Philosophy and Politics

The fate of Greek science was not shared by philosophy. For centuries the spirit of inquiry still impelled men of the highest calibre to observe, reflect, debate and seek to understand the world. The need was no less in the second or third century A.D. than it had been in the days of the Ionian physicists, and the reasons for turning to philosophy for the answers remained very similar too. Greek religion lacked dogma and systematic theology; its rituals may have been emotionally stimulating, but its explanations were always the intellectually unsatisfying ones of myth. This emptiness of religion (and the corresponding absence of an institutionalized church) gave philosophical speculation unusual freedom of manoeuvre: positively because there was a vacuum to be filled, negatively because neither men's souls nor their earthly caretakers were felt to be threatened by ideas, no matter how outrageous. The hypothesis that the earth rotates on its own axis and revolves around the sun was put forward by Strato's pupil, Aristarchus of Samos. No doubt this annoyed the gods and offended pious men, but there was no outcry. Aristarchus failed to win support on quite different grounds: the best astronomers made the valid scientific objection that the geocentric hypothesis offered a simpler explanation of the heavenly phenomena they were able to observe.

Others were less fortunate: some philosophers were hounded on charges of impiety or sacrilege, and the trial of Socrates comes immediately to mind. Indeed, it comes to mind too readily and too often, for, however one judges this by no means uncomplicated case, the brute fact remains that it was exceptional in the long history of Greek philosophy. Outbursts of genuine persecution in the city-states were infrequent and localized, the result of special conditions in one *polis* or another and therefore unlikely to spread. And often politics was found among the under-currents. Politics, in the broadest sense, impinged steadily on philosophy, interfered with it at times and always helped set its goals, indirectly if not directly. Hence the great divide in Greek politics – the time of Alexander the Great – also marks the end of one period in philosophy and the beginning of another. Many of the same questions could still be asked in the Hellenistic monarchies and the Roman Empire; many of the answers necessarily lay in new emphases and new directions.

The triumph of philosophy over science and the post-Alexandrian stress on man's inner life were both in a sense the ultimate triumph of Socrates and Plato. A revolution occurred in Greek philosophy in the second half of the fifth century, so completely identified with one man, Socrates, that his predecessors are known collectively as the 'pre-Socratics'. It would be inaccurate to believe that the earlier philosophers had wholly ignored man himself in their concentration on nature and the cosmos, just as it would be wrong to overlook altogether the contribution of Socrates' contemporaries, the much maligned sophists. Nevertheless, Socrates was without rival the catalyst of the change which placed man at the centre of philosophical inquiry. 'Know thyself', the Delphic oracle had said, and Socrates made that gnomic maxim his own, elaborating it in a number of seminal ideas: that man is capable of knowing himself by rigorous rational thought, by the dialectical method of analysis which weighs alternative hypotheses or explanations against each other; that true knowledge cannot, strictly speaking, be taught but must be apprehended for and in oneself – 'I have never been the teacher of anyone whatsoever,' Plato has him insist at his trial (*Apology* 33A); that man's knowledge of himself, of his nature, was the true end of knowledge and therefore of life – 'an unexamined life is not worth living' (*Apology* 38A); that men do evil only out of ignorance. The ultimate equation reads: Knowledge (wisdom) = virtue = happiness.

All attempts to fill out these generalizations founder because Socrates became a legendary figure within a generation. But the Socrates who matters in the end is not the man who was Plato's teacher but the Socrates who was the protagonist in many of Plato's dialogues. Whatever the actual living Socrates may have believed – and there is reason to think that he was more successful in destroying the beliefs and arguments of others than in achieving a system of his own – it was the Platonic Socrates whose questions and formulations shaped so much of western philosophy.

This Socrates believed that man's soul is the seat of his rational faculty, the essential factor which distinguishes man from the beasts. But the soul also contains an irrational element, and the great problem for man is to become truly human, that is, to allow the rational element to dominate and control the other. None of this is meaningful, furthermore, in isolation. Robinson Crusoes do not exist outside fiction. Wisdom and goodness are really possible only where there is a relationship, between man and man on the one hand, between man and the eternal on the other. Hence love, friendship, piety, immortality were among the important subjects of the

Socratic dialogues – but above all these, justice. The inquiry into justice led immediately into an analysis, and critique, of the prevailing ideas and practices of political behaviour. This step may not be inevitable in every society, but it was in the Greek city-state, with its profound community-consciousness. The *polis* was held to be the highest form of human association – 'man is by nature a *polis*-being' was how Aristotle later phrased it – and therefore it was in the *polis* that justice could be achieved if one went about it correctly.

The Greeks had had a long and complicated political experience by the time of Socrates, and they did not have to wait for him to initiate a discussion of the merits and defects of different political systems. Democracy or oligarchy, pay for office or property qualifications, local independence or empire – such questions were constantly debated, though we know little about the arguments because they were carried on orally rather than in writing. Only brief passages in writers like Solon, Herodotus and the tragedians provide some clue, as do the actual legislation and the history of political institutions. What was new about Socrates was neither political discussion as such nor the idea that politics and justice were linked, but the radical and systematic way in which the issues were examined and the unremitting insistence that politics (and all behaviour) must be rationally guided and judged by absolute ethical norms.

The Socratic approach to politics was radical in the original sense of the word: it went to the roots and began with the nature of man. It was fundamental to Plato, and to the mainstream of classical Greek philosophy after him, that men are created unequal; not merely in the superficial sense of inequality in physique, wealth or social position, but unequal in their souls, morally unequal. A few men are potentially capable of completely rational behaviour, and hence of correct moral judgement; most men are not. Therefore, government ought to be placed in the hands of the morally superior few – ideally, in the hands of the true philosophers. And their authority should be total, in scope and finality. The reason for this is rooted in Plato's metaphysics, in his notion that there are absolute goods and absolute truths, which are knowable to some men by correct education; from which it follows in simple logic that, once they are known, it is in the interest of everyone that these absolutes, and nothing else, be the standards by which men live.

This theme, or better, group of themes recurs frequently in Plato, but it found its great elaboration in the *Republic*. That is much the longest Socratic dialogue because there the search for a definition of justice involved Plato in an original and complicated analysis of the components of the soul, then of educational theory and the psychology of poetry and music, of the nature of human associations in general and the state in particular, of law and legislation, of mathematics and dialectic, with comments on property, the status of women, religion and immortality; in short, in most of the problems he recognized to be within the purview of the philosopher. The *Republic* was no blue-print (though some scholars have tried to make it one); it was a measuring-rod, a set of infallible norms towards which the good man should strive and by which existing social and political arrangements could be tested. There is one basic test for every public action and institution: Does it make men better than they were before, or not? In another dialogue, the *Gorgias* (502E–519D), Plato insisted that not even the great Athenians of the past – Miltiades, Themistocles, Cimon and Pericles – were true statesmen. They had merely been more accomplished than their successors in gratifying the desires of the *demos* with ships and walls and dockyards. They had failed to make the citizens of Athens better men, and therefore to call them 'statesmen' was to confuse the pastrycook with the doctor. This long passage embarrassed later Platonists, but only because the fire was directed against Miltiades and Pericles rather than against the fashionable targets, the 'demagogues'. Yet Plato was perfectly consistent. No existing form of *polis* was ideal, but those which stood farthest away were, indisputably, tyranny and 'extreme' democracy as practised at Athens. In the latter sovereignty lay with the morally undeserving and unqualified *demos*, whose demands and decisions were rendered still worse by the absence of a proper educational system. Therefore Athenian political leaders had no choice but to pander, like pastrycooks.

No matter how many other problems Plato turned to – and it is worth repeating Whitehead's often quoted, if hyperbolic, remark, 'European philosophical tradition . . . consists of footnotes on Plato' – he was persistently tormented by this need to make a just world. Finally, at the age of about eighty, he produced a blue-print for a state which, though decidedly not the ideal of, and in some respects even a puzzling departure from, the *Republic*, bears the unmistakable Platonic imprint throughout. The work, significantly entitled the *Laws* and longer than any other of his writings, is a massive code, in which no conceivable detail in the life of each citizen, foreigner and slave escapes regulation – not Ten Commandments but ten thousand, with carefully graded penalties for every kind of violation. Just what Plato thought he could accomplish with such a book may be unascertainable, but it is impossible to miss the fundamental implication, that so long as philosophers are not rulers the best that can be hoped for is to approximate the good life by imposing it from above, tolerating no departure, no questioning, no freedom of choice. The whole system was conceived not in the interests of, or for the benefit of, a class or party or individual, but on behalf of the state and all its members; yet it was no less a closed, authoritarian society for all its high-mindedness.

Not even the size of the population was overlooked. The total of adult male citizens was to be fixed at 5,040, a curious figure reflecting Pythagorean number-mysticism: 5,040 is the product of $1 \times 2 \times 3 \times 4 \times 5 \times 6 \times 7$. For Aristotle, who dismissed both the *Republic* and the *Laws* briefly and rather unceremoniously in the second book of his *Politics*, this proposal was a glaring example of the fallacy in Plato's method. Plato, he pointed out, neither established the machinery which would be needed to hold the number of men exactly nor realized the practical implications in property matters, among other things. The criticism is not so much that Plato missed out on a detail, but that the whole enterprise rested on false premisses. Aristotle agreed that politics were essentially an aspect of ethics – all Greek theorists held to that – but he denied that they could be meaningfully reduced to a fixed, eternal system. His own *Politics*, accordingly, was grounded in a refined analysis of existing political institutions, the raw materials having been assembled in short monographs he and his students prepared on the constitutional history of 158 states (only the one on Athens survives). The analysis is, of course, not merely descriptive; Aristotle classifies, establishes patterns of change, recommends and judges, but always with the possible in view as well as the desirable. To make one group the permanent rulers, he writes, is to invite *stasis*. And when Plato claims to be seeking the happiness of the whole state he forgets that in this respect the whole is no more than its parts; in the *Republic* no part would be happy in fact.

To support 5,040 men, furthermore, the state in the *Laws* would have to be as big as Babylon. A state like that (about which Aristotle apparently had no more precise picture than that it was monstrously large) was not viable as a community. To the end of the classical period theorists held fast to the view that the *polis* was, at least potentially, the highest form of association. Babylon and Egypt and Persia were states, of course, but not 'true states', because they lacked the elementary conditions for the good life. However much the philosophers differed on what that ideal was, they were united in seeking it within the *polis* framework.

Aristotle and the classical *polis* died at about the same time. When his contemporary, Diogenes, said, 'I am a *cosmopolites*' (citizen of the universe), he was proclaiming that citizenship had become a meaningless concept. Henceforth the search for wisdom and moral existence concentrated on the individual soul so completely that society could be rejected as a secondary and accidental factor. Diogenes' Cynic disciples claimed intellectual descent from Socrates, as did the Stoics, who became the most important philosophical school in the Hellenistic age. In that new world, Aristotle's logic and physics remained vital, not his politics or even his ethics, precisely because they were conceived as 'practical arts' within the *polis*. But Plato, paradoxically, was rescued by being de-politicalized. His rejection of the world of experience for the eternal Forms, his mysticism, his preoccupation with the soul were pre-eminently suitable for philosophies which, given the nature of Hellenistic states and society, of necessity turned man in on himself; and later for a new religious conception at the core of which was salvation. 'Know thyself' remained the motto, but with implications which would have astonished Socrates, and perhaps appalled him.

Popular Attitudes and Morals

When Socrates stood trial in 399 the clerk of the court began the proceedings by reading out the indictment: 'This affidavit is sworn to by Meletus . . . against Socrates. . . . Socrates is guilty of not believing in the gods in which the *polis* believes and of introducing other, new divinities. He is also guilty of corrupting the young. The penalty proposed is death.' The trial was completed in a single day before a jury of 501 men – all in accord with normal procedure – and he was convicted by a vote of 281 to 220.

Much remains puzzling and paradoxical about the case. Greek religion being one of ritual rather than doctrine, sacrilege too was normally a matter of acts : desecration of shrines, temple robbery, illicit participation in a rite or revealing secrets to the uninitiate, and the like. Where there is no orthodoxy there can be no heresy, and laws or prosecutions directed against a man's beliefs, not expressed in offensive actions, were rare throughout antiquity so far as we know. In Athens failure to participate in the state and household cults was normally a bar to holding the highest office in the state, the archonship, but that was about all. At the beginning of the fourth century, however, Socrates was condemned and executed for 'not believing in the gods in which the *polis* believes', though all sources agree that his piety was in fact unimpeachable.

The trouble went back at least a generation : the first victim was the outstanding scientist-philosopher Anaxagoras of Clazomenae, who saved himself from an impiety charge by fleeing to Lampsacus, where he was received with honour. The date of that affair is uncertain, as is the date of the decree of the Assembly, passed on the motion of a professional diviner named Diopeithes, forbidding the study of astronomy as sacrilegious (or the date of its abandonment, for that matter, whether by repeal or merely by desuetude). Although there is no reference to astronomy in the indictment of Socrates, Plato took pains in the *Apology* to stress Socrates' lack of interest in the subject, explicitly contrasting him with Anaxagoras. Between the two trials there were others. The story has been hopelessly corrupted by later scandal-mongering writers, but, details apart, it is clear that Athens went through a bad patch of thirty or forty years' duration, when a number of intellectuals – probably very small – were persecuted for their beliefs, rightly or wrongly interpreted. This is all the more remarkable because it seems to have been a purely Athenian phenomenon, as the reception of Anaxagoras in Lampsacus suggests, or the refuge taken for a time in Megara by some of Socrates' disciples, perhaps including Plato, after his condemnation. Whether they had reason to fear or not, the atmosphere soon changed, sharply and totally. Not later than 385 Plato founded his school in Athens, the Academy; others followed and the city rapidly became the main Greek centre for philosophy. Men came from all over to teach and study there; in later times Romans as well as Greeks. The Academy itself, it seems, maintained a continuous corporate existence until it was dissolved in A.D. 529, when the Christian emperor Justinian shut down all pagan institutions of learning.

No doubt there were political overtones. Two of the Thirty Tyrants were kinsmen of Plato's, Critias and Charmides, the latter known to be a member of the Socratic circle – Xenophon reports in detail how Socrates urged him to take up a political career. Many Athenians drew the conclusion that Socrates' teaching fostered this bloodiest chapter in the history of the Athenian democracy. But what of Anaxagoras, whose political views are unknown but who was a friend of Pericles? Or the sophist Protagoras, if the tradition is right to include him among the earlier victims of an impiety indictment, who appears to have had democratic leanings? Not to mention Plato himself, who taught and wrote freely for forty years or more, with a passionate dislike for the whole Athenian way of life that was no secret to anyone; and who did not shrink from introducing both Critias and Charmides into several dialogues in the most friendly terms.

The simple political explanation is inconsistent with the rest of Athenian behaviour in this area. The ill was more complex. Life was hard in the best of times; men were beset by inimical forces, human and supernatural. Even the Olympian gods, the source of many blessings, could punish if offended; then there were the spirits of the underworld whom not even the gods could fully control, bringers of calamity whom, in the words of Isocrates (*To Philip* 117), 'we honour neither in our prayers nor in our sacrifices, but seek to drive off'. All seemed to combine against Athens in the closing decades of the fifth century. The Peloponnesian War destroyed many lives and disrupted the lives of everyone else for years on end; it left Athens feeble, stripped of its empire, its power and glory, ground down by the Thirty Tyrants and a Spartan garrison. Many more Athenians – perhaps one-third of the population – had died in the two plagues which struck in the years 430–426. The doctors had a rational explanation but no cure; of what use, then, was their explanation? Why should one turn to them rather than to the soothsayers, oracle-mongers and magicians, who could communicate with the dark forces of the underworld and perhaps bring health and good fortune?

Nor was that all. Something new in the city's intellectual life had begun to make itself felt not many years earlier: first men like Anaxagoras came with their physics and their metaphysics, casting aside the timeless myths; then the sophists, and with them Socrates, started to challenge traditional ways of behaviour and even the laws and political arrangements as nothing better than arbitrary, and often badly chosen, conventions. In the old days sages like Solon had been revered because in their sayings and their lives they expressed hopes and ideals widely shared in the community. The new sages seemed to be doing quite the opposite, trying to tear down the accepted beliefs and values, especially in religion and morals. Their pupils and disciples, furthermore, were rich young men, members of the dining-clubs that had always been contemptuous of the democracy, or at least of the *demos*, and which seized the opportunity in the final years of the war to become conspiratorial centres for oligarchic revolution, shunning no tactic – bribery, false propaganda, terror and assassination, impious provocation – to gain their end. Athens found herself embroiled in extreme *stasis* again after a considerable period of immunity, and to many it looked as if philosophy, impiety and oligarchy were in close concert.

The ingredients were therefore present for a wild popular panic, but, near as the Athenians may have come to it at moments, none really developed; nor was there wholesale witch-hunting. There were outbursts of cruel irrational behaviour against individuals (not against classes of men), usually in response to some immediate provocation, such as the mutilation of sacred herms throughout the city one night shortly before the expedition sailed out against Sicily in 415. Others were victimized when personal grievances were exploited. Xenophon said, perhaps correctly, that Socrates was brought to trial for no better reason than the desire of Anytus, one of the accusers, to avenge a personal insult. Crude magical and superstitious practices flourished. Yet in the long run neither morale nor civic responsibility nor political stability broke down. Athens recovered quickly from the defeat and the Thirty Tyrants, and with the disappearance of the complicated war-time situation the threats to free philosophical and scientific pursuits disappeared too.

Such problems could not even have arisen in Sparta or in the backward rural states simply because they were closed to philosophers and philosophical schools altogether. Where tyrants ruled the position varied from year to year, almost from day to day, according to the tyrant's whims. What happened in late fifth-century Athens was not repeated elsewhere, for only Athens provided the necessary combination of conditions: popular sovereignty, a large and active group of vigorous original thinkers and the unique experiences brought about by the war. The very conditions, in short, which attracted the best minds in Greece to Athens could, and for a time did, put them in a singularly precarious position. Athens paid a savage penalty: the greatest Greek democracy won its greatest fame because it executed Socrates and nourished Plato, the most powerful and most radical anti-democratic moralist the world has ever known.

To strike a proper balance in judgement at this distance is enormously difficult, and probably impossible. How much influence *did* the physicists and the sophists, Socrates, Plato and Aristotle have? How deeply did the Enlightenment penetrate (as the new intellectual trend has been called on the eighteenth-century model)? Any answer which merely draws a line between 'the few' and 'the many', the educated and the uneducated, is a demonstrable over-simplification. One consequence of the plague was the introduction into Athens of the cult of Asclepius, the magical healer, whose main shrine, in Epidaurus, became a pilgrimage centre which has been compared with Lourdes. One of the god's sacred snakes was brought from Epidaurus in solemn procession. Until a temple could be erected, the snake was housed and an altar was provided for him by the playwright Sophocles on behalf of the private group sponsoring the new cult, which was soon taken over by the state as part of its religious establishment. Socrates' last words, according to Plato (*Phaedo* 118), were these: 'I owe a cock to Asclepius, Crito. You pay it without fail.'

This is not to suggest that there was no difference between Socrates and the kind of man who invoked the evil powers in a curse against some personal enemy, inscribed the curse on a lead tablet and buried it underground, preferably in a grave. The differences, however, fell within well-defined limits. Hardly any Greeks, philosophers and illiterates alike, abandoned the belief that the gods and spirits intervened in the lives of men, for good and evil, that they punished when offended, that they gave intimations – through oracles and various other devices – of their desires and intentions. Xenophanes and the atomist Democritus were perhaps exceptions, probably Thucydides and Critias, surely Epicurus (whose name became the Hebrew word for 'atheist'); but they were in this one respect altogether outside the main stream of Greek thought, without sustained influence even in advanced intellectual circles. The questions which exercised the philosophers, of all schools and tendencies, were how man should best come to terms with the unchanging conditions that bound human life, not only with the supernatural but also with existence in a community (man being by nature gregarious) and with harsh material circumstances (there being no conception of continuous technological progress); how to live happily; how to determine the correct values and norms, and then how to bring them into practice. The emphasis was almost exclusively on this life, furthermore. Even Plato, strongly influenced as he was by Pythagoreanism and perhaps by the religious movement known as Orphism, obsessed as he was with the soul, in his practical ethics was fundamentally earth-bound.

Much as the different answers conflicted, they shared a common core of rationalism, the rejection of any automatic acceptance of traditional mythical or conventional rules and explanations; the insistence that all institutions and behaviour-patterns must be justified by reference to general, 'natural' principles and norms, and that man was able, if he were prepared to make the effort, to apprehend the correct modes of behaviour. This spirit is what justifies the term Enlightenment; it is what stimulated the long outburst of sustained inquiry which was a major component of the 'Greek miracle'. Nor was it restricted to the more or less professional philosophers. The impact can be seen clearly, for example, in the development of historical writing. Hecataeus' dismissal of the 'stories the Greeks tell' as 'ridiculous' is the first available hint. In Herodotus the full force of the influence is apparent, in his persistent efforts to rationalize (or historicize) myth; in his long digressions, like the discussion between Solon and Croesus on happiness or the one he sets in the Persian court on the best form of government; in his comparisons between prevailing Greek and barbarian customs and values, in which the Greeks do not always come off best. And in Thucydides, finally, we see the philosopher *manqué*, the historian who was so familiar with current medical thought that he could match the Hippocratic writings in spirit and even in technical language in his account of the plague at Athens; who converted negotiations between an Athenian embassy and the Melians into a philosophical dialogue on might and right; who never gave up trying to fight his way from the particular and concrete to the universal.

In a different way the impact is also evident on the tragedians. To be sure, serious-minded men were perfectly capable of thinking about the gods and justice and evil without being goaded into it by philosophers, and one cannot *prove* that Aeschylus heard of, say, Xenophanes or Anaxagoras, let alone that he had studied their doctrines; any more than one can prove that Sophocles and Herodotus, who are known to have been devoted to each other, ever talked about the meaning of myths or political justice. But with Euripides, at least, we are on firm ground. Medea's final words in her great soliloquy before she kills her children (lines 1078–80), 'I know what evil I am about to do; but the *thymos* is stronger than my resolution, *thymos*, the root of man's most evil acts' (where *thymos* is her irrational self), are Euripides' reply to Socrates, his deliberate rejection of the Socratic doctrine that evil results only from ignorance. Euripides may not have been a systematic thinker, but he returned persistently to this sort of problem, and one of his last plays, the *Bacchae*, produced in

405 soon after his death, registers the complete triumph of the view that there are some forces beyond man's understanding or control which he must obey or be destroyed.

It was through such media alone that philosophical ideas and teachings percolated to a larger audience. No other means of communication were available. How much got through, and with what effect, we cannot really say. Obviously some men departed from the Theatre of Dionysus solemnly saying to their friends, in whatever was the contemporary idiomatic equivalent, 'It makes you think.' Obviously, too, there was enough blind anger abroad at this new-fangled playing about with beliefs that were good enough for our fathers. Whatever his motives, Aristophanes jumbled the physicists, sophists and Socrates together, and added comic invention of his own, in that spirit, later mocked by Plato in the *Meno*, a masterpiece of irony, when Socrates is made to defend the sophists at length against the stupid traditionalism and general know-nothingness of Anytus. No city, says the latter, ought to allow such men in. And, finally, some proportion of the population were surely ignorant of what was being taught, and indifferent.

After Euripides and Aristophanes the theatre modulated to a very minor key. After Thucydides there were still a few industrious pursuers of historical facts, but the line in that field that began with Hecataeus had come to a dead end. In human behaviour rational inquiry seemed to lead to pessimism, doubt and cynicism, not to reasonable and workable solutions. The universe was a different matter: mathematicians, astronomers and metaphysicians still had a long productive future ahead. But with respect to man himself, despite Plato, despite Aristotle, the dominant trend became a flight, whether to self-indulgence or to a blinkered concentration on the small details of daily living or to the inner life, to contemplation, indifferent to the goods and the ills alike of the physical world. Epicurus, who set up his school in 306, took upon himself the mission to remove the fear of death. Worthy as that activity was, it could not teach man how to live; more, it could be taken to imply that there was no way other than the purely negative one of preparing to die with perfect equanimity.

The flight from reality was a recognition of reality. The Greeks were now paying the price for staking everything on the *polis*-community, not merely their political organization but their livelihood, their emotional and spiritual satisfactions and protection, their values. When the *polis* proved not to be viable, when it could not sustain many of its members even on a minimum standard of living, when *stasis* and petty warfare became the rule of the day, exhortations to moral regeneration were either idle or insulting. Isocrates' kind of solution – a war of conquest and then migration – seemed far more sensible. The break-up did not come all at once, nor everywhere at the same tempo. The last days of Athenian independence showed once more how much vitality the *polis* had had. But in the end no system of internal arrangements within the *polis*, Athenian or Spartan or any other, could save that way of life. As this became increasingly apparent, though not necessarily intelligible, ideas about society and morality underwent corresponding transformations. Aristotle's empiricism in politics, his search for the possible rather than the ideal, was a last desperate attempt to shore up the dyke. It was a failure in all respects, except perhaps as a brilliant post-mortem.

How, it is then proper to ask, did all this look outside the world of books – in a society in which books played a very small and very one-sided part? Greek writers lead us to exaggerate the preoccupation with politics, a tendency to which we are prone anyway because of modern, especially nineteenth-century, historiographical habits. It is probably true that politics involved and concerned more people more of the time among the Greeks than in most later periods of history.

Nevertheless, that would be the case only for Athens and other vigorously democratic *poleis*, and even there not for a sizeable portion of the citizenry (themselves a minority of the inhabitants). Much as we know about the Greeks at work and play, in the family and the village, the direct evidence is largely about the external aspects alone, without clear perspective or balance between different kinds of activity, without forthright indications of the connexions with religion or politics or poverty. The fourth century, for example, seems to have been marked by a growth in mystery and orgiastic cults and in magical practices, and towards the end by the rise of Tyche, Luck or Fortune, from a not very important female spirit to perhaps the favourite of all divinities for private (but not public) appeals. But one must say 'seems', because there is no documentary, let alone statistical, proof of a significant quantitative growth (except in the case of Tyche); and one may then infer that the trend was the popular response – the substitute for a philosophical reaction – to the loss of the sustaining power of the *polis* and therefore of its traditional patron deities.

The whole subject of private morality is beset with such difficulties. The pivotal role of the family cannot be doubted. It was the primary institution through which most of life was organized and continuity assured: in the management and inheritance of property, in providing citizens in each new generation (hence the overriding interest of the state in questions of legitimacy), in the day-to-day relations with the gods, in transmitting and instilling the moral code. Yet the family does not bulk large in most Greek writing, its affective and psychological sides hardly at all.

Two factors, not unrelated, were at work. One was class. When Plato proposed in the *Republic* that the family should be abolished among the philosopher-rulers because it was an impediment to their acting as perfect moral agents, or when

Aristotle argued in the eighth book of the *Ethics* that true friendship is possible only between equals, so that the relationship between man and woman is of a lower order, each was translating into his own terms the actual behaviour-patterns on the social level on which he lived. In the upper classes one did not *live* in the family in the sense of finding companionship there. For that one went to other men or to other women, usually to both, and companionship was physical and spiritual together. The whole situation is perfectly summed up in the vocabulary. *Hetairos* is an old Greek word for 'comrade-in-arms', a term of the military aristocracy. It emerges in classical Athens as *hetaireia*, the upper-class dining-club, very likely made up of members of the same age-group; but also as *hetaira*, a 'courtesan' (not to be confused with a *pornē*, a common prostitute). Pederasty was a feature of military *élites*, as in Sparta and Thebes, and in other communities of the upper classes (and therefore of the intellectual *élite*). Homosexuality, the direction of sexual impulses solely to members of the same sex, was something quite different, the object of contempt and malicious jokes. The normal pattern was a bisexuality, so that two complementary institutions co-existed, the family taking care of what we may call the material side, pederasty (and the courtesan) the affective, and to a degree the intellectual, side of a man's intimate life.

For the lower and middle classes the evidence is both sparse and confused, but perhaps the right interpretation is that, though bisexuality was accepted throughout the society, institutionally the family tended to monopolize the field. That means, further, that as the society in a place like Athens became more 'middle class', speaking in terms of social psychology and not in the modern sense, with its economic implications, in Menander's kind of world, in other words, institutionalized pederasty, rooted in the archaic aristocracy, increasingly lost its place. One obvious factor pulling in that direction was poverty, leaving men little leisure and no money to spend, while it gave their wives, whose labour on farms and in shops was indispensable, a measure of equality. In one respect, however, the unequal relationship never changed: both in law and in practice there was a double standard of sexual morality. This can be seen in its simplest terms in the narrow, one-sided definition of adultery, which never meant anything other than sexual intercourse between a married woman and a man not her husband. The offence, it need hardly be added, was against the husband, just as rape or seduction was an offence against the father or guardian, not against the woman.

Considerations of status, property, affection or love do not exhaust the question. Sex and fertility were a mystery, too; the Oedipus story was not an invention of Sigmund Freud's after all. Reading the great classical authors, however, reveals very little of this magical side of sex, and that – the rationalist and rationalizing tendency – is the second major source of distortion. One must go to the writers, mostly late ones, who were interested in collecting the details of myths and rites, ʌnd to the remains of ritual regulations, and then one will amass a remarkable collection of beliefs and practices linking sex and religion: transvestite and fetishistic practices, sacred virginity, sexual taboos imposed on priests and priestesses, priapic rites. The psychology in this area of behaviour was obviously not the simple, frank, child-like recognition of a natural function that is so often assumed from the easy obscenity of Aristophanes or the eroticism in works of art, but something very ambiguous, potent and dangerous at the same time, a power that came from beyond man and could, if properly manipulated, be used by him to control the forces of nature and the underworld, to ward off evil or ensure his crops. Nor were these beliefs restricted to the uneducated and the 'superstitious'. The mutilation perpetrated on the herms in Athens in 415 consisted in breaking off the erect phalli of the statues, and herms were not a phenomenon of the Athenian slums.

The conclusion which emerges is the obvious one that it was Euripides, not Socrates – the Euripides of the *Bacchae* – who captured the actual psychology and values of his contemporaries. They did not see a choice between reason and passion, Apollo and Dionysus, the eternally perfect and the corrupt transitory, but the necessity of living with both, with all the resulting ambiguity and uncertainty. And 'they' means nearly all Greeks, though the balance moved to one side or the other in different degrees. Distinctions of class or education were important, but it was no more the case with the Greeks than with any other people that there were two (or more) distinct sets of value systems, that there was a civilized minority who lived the life of reason and a superstitious, barbarous majority. The gap between the extremes was enormous, and the continuing attraction of the Greeks rests largely on their efforts to free themselves from magic and darkness. But the overlapping areas were very large as well, and in terms of their lives and their fate, perhaps decisive.

There could be no better example than the attitudes to slavery. This was a universal institution among the Greeks, one that touched upon every aspect of their lives without exception. It rested on very fundamental premises, of human inequality, of the limits of authority and debasement, of rights and rightlessness. By chance there has been preserved a large section of the accounts for the final stages of the building of the Erechtheum on the Acropolis in the years 409–404. The status of 86 workmen is known: 20 slaves, 24 citizens, 42 metics. This was the stage when some of the most delicate stone-carving, woodwork and decorative painting were being done (Plates 10 and 11), and the slaves performed their share of it (not one of them was an unskilled labourer). In most cases their owners were also on the job with them. What was the psychology, then, of Phalakros, citizen of Athens, while he and his three slaves, all stone-masons, were being employed by the state to do this work, and in this respect were equals in the eyes of the state, but in no other respect? Or what was the psychology of the free men of Corcyra when their civil war erupted in 427 and both sides appealed to the slaves for armed support in the fighting? What was the slave's psychology?

It is doubtful whether satisfactory answers can be given. Merely to transfer what is known from modern experience, which means chiefly that of the southern states of the United States, gets it largely wrong for a number of reasons, the most important probably being the absence of the colour distinction in antiquity and the frequency of manumission. The latter both gave the slaves an incentive, a future, and gave everyone the problem of resolving the contradiction between a slave population and a growing ex-slave population. It is also doubtful that most Greeks ever gave the matter serious thought. The philosophers, however, could not avoid the question, and their attempt to come to terms with it was perhaps the greatest of their failures.

If slavery were to be justified at all, it could only be on the lines laid down by Aristotle in the first book of the *Politics*. Many, he argued, are slaves by nature; therefore it is natural, and in their own interest, that they be subject to men who could make the necessary moral judgements for them. He went further and categorized all barbarians as slaves by nature. And this generalization destroyed the whole theory (as Aristotle himself seems eventually to have appreciated), for it was contrary to easily observed experience. Some philosophers had challenged the natural theory of slavery earlier, and after Aristotle it had few defenders. But what was to replace it? Nothing better was available than two poor alternatives. Either one held that slavery, though contrary to nature, was a conventional status universally recognized, and justified on that ground; or one held that a man's social and legal status – slavery or freedom – was unimportant, since only the state of the soul mattered. No one in antiquity seriously put forward a third view, namely, that slavery should be abolished because it was morally wrong.

CHAPTER 7

THE VISUAL ARTS

THE complicated interplay between local autonomy and pan-Hellenism was brought into sharpest focus in the visual arts. On the one hand, every *polis* had the same needs as every other; there was no metropolis or cathedral town, so that the difference between Thebes, for example, and a tiny place like Plutarch's native Chaeronea in Boeotia was one of scale only. On the other hand, despite many local variations, there was a remarkable uniformity of tastes and wants, changing in time rather than in place. This is evidenced in many ways: in the rapid diffusion of the Doric temple throughout mainland and western Greece; in the ease with which leading architects and sculptors moved about; or, in the private sphere, in the dominating position maintained by Athenian fine painted pottery throughout the Greek world for two centuries or more. One need not exaggerate such phenomena, but the fact remains that a classical Greek found himself in a relatively familiar environment, in this respect, wherever he travelled.

This universality reflected, and was fostered by, the very close link between the arts and the community. Classical Greece was a world almost completely without palaces or private mansions. On the island of Delos archaeologists have in recent years uncovered luxurious, richly decorated, two-storey houses built for the Italian merchants who came there in the second and first centuries B.C. after Rome had conquered the eastern Mediterranean and converted the island into a centre for maritime trade. It had long been a great pan-Hellenic shrine, filled with temples and statuary, but it had to wait for the Romans to put up private housing of comparable splendour. Greek architecture, even sculpture and painting, were public arts in the strict sense. Of the public buildings, the temple and later (and to a lesser degree) the theatre, both directly and immediately connected with cult, outranked all others. There were altars everywhere, in the gates, in the assembly-places, in the streets, but neither the meeting-place on the Pnyx in Athens nor the Council-House was, properly speaking, a religious building, and neither was conceived, aesthetically or otherwise, in the same class as the Parthenon or the Erechtheum. This is not to denigrate secular public buildings, for the Greeks lavished much care on them, as they did on such small objects as coins (Plate 8); but they had a scale of values which elevated the temple above other buildings, as it elevated the great statues of Athena or Zeus above all other sculpture.

The state was therefore almost the sole patron of the monumental arts. Given the nature of the classical *polis*, this meant neither individual rulers (except in the west, where tyrants remained important) nor professional fine-arts commissions, but the community acting through its usual instrumentalities, the assemblies, councils and magistrates. The same men who levied taxes and approved peace treaties also ordered, supervised, maintained and paid for public works. Art was meshed in with daily living, not set apart for occasional leisure-time or for the special enjoyment of rich collectors and aesthetes. Art was found in the temples, theatres, stoas and cemeteries, not in museums. At home, too, there were beautiful coins and beautiful water-jugs and drinking-cups, cosmetic jars, mirrors and jewellery, terra-cotta dolls for children – rather than *objets d'art*. There were no family portraits, no busts, but upon his death a man (or even his wife or his child) might have a sculpted tombstone of marble (Plate 12); never did an exception prove the rule more completely.

To be sure, many could not afford fine painted pottery and made do with cheap plain ware, just as many were buried under roughly hewn field-stones or inferior, mass-produced gravestones. Nor were the communities uninfluenced by finances: the number and size of their temples and theatres obviously depended on their resources, and sometimes the quality. Finances apart, not every temple or statue turned out to be a great work of art, any more than every play or choral ode, every vase or gravestone. There were even whole areas of persistently poor stuff, like the south Italian pottery manufactured in direct imitation of the Athenian. Yet, risky and subjective as it may be to say so, one has the strong impression that in all fields the quality – at least down to the fourth century – was remarkably high, the proportion of incompetent, unsuccessful and ugly work relatively small, though not to be overlooked. This sustained level of excellence was more than a matter of a high standard of craftsmanship, though it required good craftsmen; it developed, so far as we know, without any articulated aesthetic theory; that came later and was the work of philosophers rather than of artists; it was marked by a canonical quality which somehow escaped uniformity, monotony leading to sterility and general decline.

Much of the canonical impression which is so immediate to the observer is ultimately mathematical. Long before Plato, even before Pythagoras perhaps, the notion became entrenched in the arts that number was the key to harmony. Thus the Doric temple is made up of carefully considered, often simple ratios, that, for instance, between the height of the columns and the spaces between their axes; there were rules of proportion in sculpture, as for the two perpendicular lines, one from nipple to nipple, the other the length of the torso; and pottery had various standards of its own. Out of this general notion and the rules to which it gave rise there emerged clear-cut types, whether of temples or male figures or water-jugs. In pottery, Rhys Carpenter has said, 'species appear and maintain themselves with the most startling definiteness of shape', so that 'one comes to believe in their real objective existence'. Artists worked within a clear and understood framework; their clients and patrons, in turn, knew beforehand what they were getting. On neither side was there the restless search or demand for new and highly individual styles and conceptions so familiar in our own day. Among the Greeks it was the philosopher who occasionally played the role of outsider or rebel, not the artist. He expressed the accepted values of the society; he neither stood apart from them nor fought against them.

This can also be said of the Egyptians, which means that it does not say enough about the relationship between the Greek artist and his work, between the artist and his community. One need only look at the series of great archaic sculptures of male nudes known as *kouroi*: the earliest betray their Egyptian inspiration at once, but in less than a century Greek sculptors had developed them in a way no Egyptian achieved, or even tried so far as we know, in two thousand years (Plate 5). Like the poets from Archilochus on, like the physicists, the artists were also distinct personalities. It is true that the language had no word which separated the artist or 'art' from the craftsman and 'craft', but too much can be made of that fact. Sculptors, potters and painters early acquired the habit of signing their work – a revolutionary step in the history of art. They were individuals, but not individualists. They accepted the framework and the canons and then explored their possibilities freely and fully, bringing their skills, their imagination and inventiveness to play in every detail. It can be shown that not a single major line in the Parthenon is absolutely straight, its spacings often not quite equal. That is how Ictinus created the greatest of all Doric temples. Outbursts of 'originality', radical departures were very rare – the Erechtheum is an outstanding example (Plate

10) – and they were either accepted or rejected quickly, every-where, with the astonishing speed so often noticed in Greek history (the Phoenician alphabet, when finally adopted by the Greeks, and coined money being two familiar instances). Yet growth, movement, vitality, standards of excellence con-tinued, in some fields more than others, for a very long time.

Inevitably the social and political transformations in the Hellenistic and Roman periods brought about enormous changes in art as well. Much patronage was now that of autocratic monarchs and tyrants, sometimes of wealthy pri-vate benefactors. This may still be called, technically, state patronage – and Hellenistic monarchs openly employed their patronage for political purposes both internally and abroad – but at heart it was individual. In a sense, the individual now displaced the community at the centre of attention through-out the society. On the royal level this was expressed in greater and greater size and more and more ornateness, to demonstrate the splendour and power of the patron. In the second half of the third century Hiero II of Syracuse built a stone altar near the theatre for the feast of Zeus Eleutherios, more than 200 yards in length, 25 yards wide, with special ramps at both ends up which the sacrificial animals were led. The Great Altar of Pergamum, commissioned by Eumenes II in the next century, is a quadrilateral 112 × 120 feet, with two magnificent continuous friezes, the outer one alone measuring 446 feet (Plate 24). In the private sphere the new individual-ism found an outlet in more expensive private houses and in portrait sculpture (Plate 23). Few students speak any longer of a complete decline in Greek art in the Hellenistic age; it would be difficult, however, to deny that there had been fundamental changes, often clearly foreshadowed in the fourth century.

Architecture and City-Planning

The Greek countryside was filled with people, but architecturally empty. Except for occasional temple-complexes which developed at a distance from the cities, significant building was concentrated in the centres. As time went on, furthermore, they became so crowded that a cluttered appearance was the rule. City walls were strong but irregular, with gates often unrelated to the main interior arteries (in sharp contrast to medieval towns). Streets were narrow and crooked. The public square, the Agora, tended to become a chaos around the edges as one new building was squeezed in after another, market-stalls encroached and statuary and dedicatory stone plaques were put up everywhere. Athens is a fair example: apart from the retention of an unpaved open area of about ten acres in the centre, there is no discernible single idea behind her Agora architecture. Or the clutter at Delphi, where the Sacred Way that wound up the hill to the main temple of Apollo was lined with dedicatory objects and buildings, accumulating century after century while some of the old ones crumbled and a few were pulled down.

The gilt statue of [the courtesan] Phryne was the work of Praxiteles, who was her lover; the statue was dedicated [to Apollo] by Phryne herself. Next in order are two statues of Apollo, one dedicated by the Argolid Epidaurians from Persian booty, the other by the Megarians to commemorate a victory over Athens near Nisaea. The ox was dedicated by the Plataeans on the occasion when they, together with the other Hellenes, drove off [the Persian general] Mardonius son of Gobryas from their territory. Then there are two more statues of Apollo. . . .

So wrote Pausanias in the second century A.D., in his *Description of Greece* (X 15, 1), and most of the monuments in this brief excerpt were erected in the fifth century B.C. Clearly nothing could be more unhistorical than the neatly cleared and landscaped sites which have been left as showpieces after some modern excavations have been completed. The reality was often (though not always) a clash: wonderfully harmonious proportions in the single building hand in hand with a lack of balance and harmony, whether aesthetic or functional, in the grouping of the buildings.

The idea of a regular plan is attributed in the Greek tradition to a man named Hippodamus, a Milesian, who flourished in the middle of the fifth century. Even though archaeologists have recently found the rectangular gridiron system to be much earlier, in Old Smyrna not later than the seventh century and perhaps in some western colonies too, the tradition was effectively accurate: Aristotle knew what he was saying when he spoke of 'the new, Hippodamean fashion'. Small colonial settlements on virgin soil were not the model of how most Greek cities actually grew. Hippodamus appeared as a reformer, a planner (and also a utopian political theorist), and he was apparently given some opportunity to put his ideas into practice in the Piraeus (the port of Athens) and perhaps elsewhere. Resistance was strong and for a time successful. His approach was too abstract and formally mathematical, with little relationship to the terrain, highly irregular as it usually was, or to the way Greeks lived and functioned. Among other things, as Aristotle pointed out (*Politics*, VII 1330b), there were grave objections from a military viewpoint: the old haphazard arrangement of streets and buildings always confused and hampered invaders, either in trying to get in or in trying to fight their way out. And in general the city-states had neither the finances nor the organization with which to carry out such schemes. They built as they went along, depending on their circumstances and moods and on the state of the treasury at any given time.

A late foundation like Olynthus, developed in the second

half of the fifth century on the north-eastern fringe of the Aegean area, is a rare instance of a classical city with a regular layout. But again it was the Hellenistic age which saw the decisive change, the triumph of planned regularity, heralded, as it were, with the re-siting of Priene in Asia Minor, which began just before Alexander. When one examines Hellenistic plans a little more carefully another feature of striking significance emerges. The Agora was now closed off on all four sides, as if to proclaim by this single architectural development that free movement and assemblage of the people were a thing of the past. Not only was this the rule in the new foundations of Hellenistic monarchs and tyrants, but it spread to the old Greek world as well. In Athens the building which marks the new era most dramatically is the two-storied stoa, more than 125 yards in length, donated by Attalus II, king of Pergamum from 159 to 138 (brother and successor of Eumenes II). From simple beginnings, the stoa had become gigantic, filled with shops at the rear, the dominant building in the Agora.

Yet even the stoa of Attalus was in its elements a purely *Greek* building. The combination of solid walls at the rear and sides and the rows of columns, open and regularly spaced, along the front, the rectangular layout, the roofing-over of the whole structure and the abundance of sculpture in the bays – these elements made up Greek architecture, so to speak. From about 600 on, the normal temple was a rectangle, with a solid-walled and roofed centre (the *cella*) in which the statue of the divinity and a miscellany of dedicated objects and treasure were stored, and an outer frame of columns, also roofed. From the seventh century, too, it was the practice to construct public buildings of stone. Marble, abundant in Greece in a variety of shades and textures, came into extensive use in the sixth century, but only in the fifth, and then rarely, for the whole of large buildings (as on the Athenian Acropolis). Limestone remained the most common material. The roofs were either wood or clay tile, occasionally marble. Much paint was used on the mouldings and elsewhere, preferably in reds, blues and other bright colours. Brick was generally reserved for private buildings, a poor material (sundried) for poor and unimportant architecture.

Nowhere is the canonical character of Greek art more clear-cut than in its temples, both in the limits and in the flexibility within the limits. Barring exceptions, temples are chiefly distinguished by 'order', Doric or Ionic (Plates 14 and 15). The latter is both lighter and more elaborate, treating the bases and capitals of the columns more decoratively, with corresponding differences in the friezes, with a different architectural rhythm, less square and mathematical in its impact. (The so-called Corinthian order is not an independent one at all, merely a more ornate off-shoot of the Ionic and of little importance until Roman times in any case.) Within each order, despite the often wonderful variations in detail, there was an essential sameness about temples for centuries on end. The Parthenon was not only the greatest triumph; it was also the end-point, many years before the close of the fifth century. Painting and sculpture had already undergone considerable change, and were to continue to do so, but architecture generally rested in the framework established fairly early in the archaic period.

For the temple, at least, there were two binding factors which were closely connected: the religious practice of the Greeks and their out-of-doorness. Since the temples were not places of worship, their architects, unlike the builders of medieval cathedrals, were not impelled to reach to the heavens or to cater for the physical and emotional needs of large assemblages of the devout. Temples were designed solely to be looked at from the outside; not until Hellenistic palaces and villas were built did Greek architects concern themselves much

with interiors. In this respect nothing could be more misleading than our usual impression: we see ruins, we look through
them, we walk about *inside* the Parthenon or the temples at
Paestum. What Greeks saw was physically quite different,
apart from all the psychological and emotional associations,
and they were satisfied to cling to the square, right-angled
structure punctuated by columns. To be sure, they also built
in the round, occasionally in small temples, most notably
in their theatres. Vertically, however, they never departed
from the column or straight wall topped by flat coverings.
They used neither the arch nor the vault, long known to the
Babylonians and the Egyptians and widely employed by
them, though normally in brick. The Greeks disliked brick,
and the stone arch is a far more complicated matter. Perhaps,
then, the suggestion that the Greeks were 'timid engineers'
explains why their architecture moved towards greater size
and greater ornateness, when it moved at all, rather than to
new conceptions and forms. Or perhaps the answer is more
psychological, an inertia, the absence of any drive to do things
otherwise. Either way, it was left to the Romans to explore
the possibilities of the arch and the vault, and later the dome,
and thereby to enrich architecture, using brick and then concrete as the appropriate materials.

Sculpture

In rebuilding after the Persian invasion the Athenians first
developed the Agora and ignored the Acropolis. The choice
was no doubt motivated by the urgency of getting daily life
back on an orderly footing, perhaps by limited funds. But it is
tempting to see a psychological reason as well, expressed in a
well-known and well-founded generalization by Aristotle
(*Politics*, VII 1330b): 'A citadel (acropolis) is suitable to oli-

garchy and one-man rule, level ground to democracy.' In less than a generation, however, the position was altered. The triumphant, rich, self-confident and imperialist democracy, led by Pericles, returned to the Acropolis, which was a venerable site, and they made of it not only their greatest religious centre but also the visible symbol of Athenian power and glory. The man in charge of the programme, at least unofficially, was Pheidias, the most famous of all Greek sculptors, a native Athenian who executed important commissions in many places, including Delphi, Thebes and Olympia. Unfortunately it is far from clear exactly how much of the work on the Acropolis was actually his. The architects for the Parthenon (Plate 14) were Ictinus and Callicrates. Who its sculptors were is unknown; obviously there were many, but one man was surely responsible for the conception and design. Although that may well have been Pheidias, there is no certain proof.

What the career of Pheidias exemplified perfectly was the very special link between sculpture and architecture (to the degree that the sculptor could be the dominant figure on a project). Statues in and before temples or in tombs and palaces, elaborately carved capitals on columns, sculpted gate-posts and lintels – one or another of such features had a history in the Aegean stretching back for centuries, in Egypt and the Middle East for millennia. But the Greeks introduced something totally new, which by itself was sufficient to give their temples a character unmatched elsewhere. They attached sculpture to the structure as an integral element, from elegant mouldings and decorated antefixes (Plates 11 and 4c) to the metopes, friezes and pediments (Plates 9, 13 and 16) in which artists were not only able to portray the individual figures of mythology but went on to intricate, imaginative groupings and to narration. Though the buildings themselves became a relatively fixed frame, furthermore, the reliefs kept pace with developments in free-standing statues well into the Hellenistic age, as on the Pergamene altar (Plate 24). This is the same phenomenon witnessed at the other end of the scale, on coins. There the frame had no elasticity at all. Yet the freshness of the engraving, in a profusion of subjects and themes, seems never ending; Greek coins are without parallel, and any *polis*, league or kingdom, no matter how small, managed to find first-rate artists to design and mint its coins when it wished (Plate 8).

It would be almost true, but not quite, to say that all Greek sculpture to the end of the fifth century (and much of it thereafter) was directly associated with religion. In temples the themes were religious as a matter of course. But outside, too, the connexions were more common than may at first sight seem the case. It would be wrong, for example, to think of the many statues of athletes, such as the bronze charioteer at Delphi (Plate 6), as a genuine exception. After all, the charioteer was set up in the great pan-Hellenic shrine, as a dedication to Apollo. Athletics were an integral part of religious festivals; the Greeks thought it natural to celebrate the gods by feats of prowess along with beautiful poems, noble sentiments, sacrifices and prayers. Statues of the victors, like choral odes, were a thanksgiving by the community (or tyrant) they represented. Like the odes, too, the statues were not really concerned with the athletes as individuals; they were in no sense portraits but ideal types, and it is of the greatest significance that the same type was employed indiscriminately for men and gods. The familiar archaic statues of young nude males are sometimes labelled 'Apollo' and sometimes 'Youth' (Plate 5), a distinction which is possible only when there is external evidence, if the statue is funerary, for example, or if the base survives with an inscribed text.

The nude, in Sir Kenneth Clark's words, 'is an art form invented by the Greeks . . . just as opera is an art form invented in seventeenth-century Italy'. Its roots lay very deep, in the aristocratic psychology and habits of the archaic era, the age when the practice began of competing naked in the games, singled out by Thucydides and other writers as one of the distinguishing marks separating Greeks from barbarians. As an art-form the nude was for more than a century only the male nude. The female nude made a hesitant appearance in the fifth century (Plate 17), but did not really flourish until the following centuries, and always with restrictions. Male gods, whether Apollo, Zeus, Poseidon or anyone else, were regularly portrayed in the nude; of the goddesses, only Aphrodite. A wife might have a funeral monument; Phryne had her statue in Delphi. That this pattern in the history of art was closely bound up with the pattern in the history of sexual relations – specifically with the social roles of pederasty and the courtesan – seems undeniable. It is equally undeniable that there were erotic overtones in these sculptures, even in the most archaic, mixed in with the religious. In a sense the work of art had become autonomous, at the same time that it retained its intimate connexion with the various social functions and activities which it served. There could be no better example of the Greek refusal to compartmentalize their ideas: the line between the secular (in its ideal expression) and the religious, between the physical and the spiritual, between human love and divine, between rest and motion, was not sharp in sculpture any more than in other forms of expression.

To the modern eye the archaic sculptures have an unmistakably hieratic flavour, but not the classical any longer. In part the change in effect was the result of growing mastery over the material, stone and bronze, and of more accurate detailed knowledge of the human body. But there was more to it. Artists were not outside the intellectual atmosphere of their time, and their religion, unlike (say) Egyptian, gave them scope to explore. They, too, strove to find and express the ideal, and they believed the road to lie through mathematical proportions. Hence the famous paradox attributed by Pliny the Elder (*Natural History*, XXXIV 65) to Lysippus of Sicyon, the favourite sculptor of Alexander and with Praxiteles the greatest master of the new naturalistic style that developed in the fourth century: 'He often said that they [the earlier artists] represented men as they really are, but he as they appeared to be.' Much of the history of Greek sculpture can be written in mathematical terms, expressing the ratios within the various elements of the human figure and their relationships to each other, conceived as so many planes rather than solids. For until the later fourth century statues were designed to be viewed frontally, with regular silhouettes at the four cardinal points, front, back and sides. As with temples, the tendency was for repetition and order, the individual genius of the sculptor finding its outlet in nuances, not radical innovation. The tendency, fortunately, never became an iron law; sculptures were not frozen in the psychology of archaism, or of fifth-century classicism; they moved, often by imperceptible steps, to meet the challenge of new conceptions and of changing demands.

Apart from architectural sculpture, large classical statues are known today almost entirely from numerous Roman copies. Bronze, in particular, was too valuable to be left standing for ever when it could be melted down, and it is only the accidental recovery in recent years of a few masterpieces from the sea (Plate 7) and from several excavations that has given us an accurate idea of large classical bronzes. The Romans had a passion for Greek statuary (many Roman emperors had themselves and their favourites depicted as Greek gods and heroes), and by the beginning of the first century, at the latest, they were able to make first-class copies by the method known as 'pointing'. The trouble with our dependence on copies is not that they are not good enough – some are, despite much incompetent work and deliberate modification – but that the process is selective according to later tastes. One type of statue in particular has disappeared so completely, apart from brief literary descriptions or reproductions on coins, that the total impression of classical Greek sculpture is distorted if it is restricted to what can actually be seen in existing collections.

In antiquity Pheidias was most praised for his 'chryselephantine' statues of Athena (in the *cella* of the Parthenon) and of Zeus (in Olympia). The descriptive adjective merely means 'covered with gold and ivory', which they were in great quantity, but it is hard to avoid the nasty pun inherent in the English word, for these statues were truly colossal. So was another of his Athenas, the Promachos, a bronze colossus which took nine years to complete and which towered above the Parthenon and the Erechtheum, between which it stood (according to a representation on Athenian coins of the Roman period). In one respect, therefore, sculpture was caught up in the contradictions of anthropomorphism. The more the figure of a god was idealized, the more indistinguishable it became from man; the one alternative which would leave a stamp of unmistakable divinity was to pull the size far out of human reach. Unlike the Romans, the classical Greeks on the whole avoided the architectural megalomania of the Colosseum, but they could not altogether escape it in the idols of the *sanctum sanctorum*.

Subsequent trends reflected not so much new developments in religion as the changing relationship between the individual and the community, culminating in the replacement of the world of the *poleis* by the Hellenistic. Depiction of the ideal did not stop, but it became increasingly unsatisfying to the sculptor's patrons. The secularism which first began to show itself in sculpture in the late fifth century became more and more marked as the years went on, and with it the subordination of the ideal type to the individual personality (Plate 23).

Politicians, orators, even writers and philosophers were honoured with statues which were actual portraits, and in the Hellenistic age, of course, kings and their consorts. Departure from the ideal also brought the trivial into art – one is reminded of New Comedy – not only in terra-cotta *objets d'art* (Plate 18), but even in marble and bronze, in the choice of subject and in the manner of treatment. Not even the gods and heroes were immune: they now became individuals as they had always been in the old heroic poems, but not in tragedy and not previously in the monumental arts. The Hellenistic Aphrodites are women who feel shame and love, who are unmistakable individuals in a way that no classical statue ever was.

Painting

The colour which was liberally applied to Greek statues and buildings is nearly all lost in the surviving remains. So too is the colour which decorated the walls of stoas, temples and Hellenistic palaces. And so are the panel paintings. The history of Greek painting must therefore be written from one not altogether fair example, pottery, and otherwise from remarks in the literature and from inference.

Well-shaped painted pottery had a continuous history in Greece from early Bronze Age days, long before the Mycenaean period – a history unmatched among contemporary peoples and probably among any other people anywhere. The Dark Age was felt here, too, but pottery was the first of the arts to recover. Perhaps by the year 1000, with Athens in the lead, first-rate pottery began to reappear, some of it soon monumental in scale, decorated only by geometric designs. When human figures were later introduced they, too, were so elongated, stylized and 'unrealistic', and grouped in such a fashion that they were extensions of the geometric pattern more than human intrusions (Plate 19). Subsequent developments became very complicated, for technique, shape and decoration all advanced greatly, and different Greek centres played different, and highly individual, roles in the process. Painted utility pottery was universal with the Greeks, wherever they migrated. Some of it was also exported to their barbarian neighbours; the Etruscans and other peoples of Italy imported it in great quantity and manufactured imitations in great quantity, too; but the civilized eastern peoples never showed the slightest interest in it. More curious still, though Greek cities always manufactured their own cheap pots, most of them eventually decided to leave the finer products in very few hands, at first Corinth, and after the middle of the sixth century almost exclusively Athens.

It is no denigration of the quality and craftsmanship of Corinthian pottery to say that the painting was purely decorative, in the sense in which the finest wall-papers or cloths are decorative (Plate 22). The pottery was intended for use – it is remarkable how rarely one finds among the innumerable Greek vases and pitchers and cups a nonfunctional, eccentric object – and it was therefore decorated in order to make it pleasing, not to convert the object into a wall or canvas on which to paint a 'work of art'. Somehow, and whatever the explanation, the Athenians then succeeded in pushing this notion as far as it could go. They excelled in covering the curved surfaces with scenes, often in complicated compositions. In the first phase, reaching its climax during the tyranny of Peisistratus, black paint was used on the clay background, which, when fired, was predominantly orange in colour, though ranging towards yellow in one direction or towards red in the other in any given pot (Plate 20). Then, near the end of the sixth century, the technique was 'invented' of reversing the process, blacking out the background and leaving the actual 'painting' in the colour of the clay (Plate 21). The new style is conventionally known as 'red-figured' and the earlier one as 'black-figured'. Within two decades or so, red-figured ware took over completely and the other virtually ceased.

A feeling for appropriateness seldom deserted Athenian potters and their painters. Just as the shapes of the objects, for all the many variations, were nicely adjusted to their function, so the painting was kept in balance with the curved space – and up to a point, with the ultimate use. Much pottery was used in connexion with religion, whether to be buried in graves or to contain oil for libations, and the designs were appropriate: funeral scenes or bits of mythology and the like. But the majority of the objects were made for ordinary personal use, and then there were no limits to the themes, running from the mythological and military to the domestic, the ribald, the grotesque and the obscene. Painters of pots had a freedom, in this respect, which was denied to sculptors, and they used it with joyful abandon and wonderful imagination. Their limitation was another one, inherent in the material itself. The paintings were lacking in depth, and ultimately in significant variety. Though some colours were added, and in the fifth century very beautiful jars and jugs were made with a white-slip background (giving a quite different effect from the reds and blacks), the range remained restricted, and a certain monotony becomes unmistakable. That effect was heightened by the persistent use of line drawing for all the figures, eliminating the element of shading with its many possibilities.

Here and there one detects efforts to transcend the limitations, clearly under the influence of mural and panel painting. The future of Greek painting lay with the latter, not in pottery (late in the fourth century painted figurative pottery came to an end), but the evidence is lost. Indirect clues exist, however, and they suggest, first, that mural painting was very common, probably beginning along with the revival of monumental architecture; second, that it was restricted on the whole to public buildings, including, in the Hellenistic age, royal palaces; third, that its development was much slower than that of architecture or sculpture; fourth, that gradually the painters learned how to model figures with light and shade, and how to create the illusion of three dimensions. Although the names of renowned fifth-century painters survive, the greatest name was Apelles, who flourished a century later than Pheidias. He was Alexander's court-painter. The juxtaposition is compelling: the greatest sculptor was most closely identified with Pericles, the greatest painter with the conqueror and monarch who initiated the Hellenistic age.

CHAPTER 8

THE HELLENISTIC AGE

THE northernmost parts of the Greek peninsula were occupied by kindred peoples whose evolution failed to keep pace with that of the Greeks themselves. In the fifth century Epirus and Macedon were still conglomerations of tribes, living on agriculture and pasturage, held together more or less firmly by kings. Court circles, especially in Macedon, maintained military and economic contacts with the Greek world, and the upper classes became more and more Greek in their culture. With the accession of Philip II to the Macedonian throne in 359, the whole picture changed rapidly and decisively. He first established his position in Macedon securely, reorganized the army and improved its equipment and tactics, making it much the best force of the time. By a single-minded combination of war and diplomacy, he then proceeded to make himself master of Greece with the intention of mounting a joint invasion of the Persian Empire. Philip was assassinated in 336, before that undertaking could be begun, but his twenty-year-old son Alexander swiftly put down an attempt by a few Greek cities to reassert their independence, and then carried out the conquest of the Persians and further incursions into India with a genius which became legendary in his own lifetime.

Alexander died in 323, ruler of Macedon, Greece, western Asia and Egypt, a god on earth (having been hailed as the son of Zeus by the priests of Zeus-Ammon in a famous shrine in the Libyan desert). His short life had been spent entirely in campaigns. If he had any long-range programme, whether for the organization of his empire or for future conquests or for the succession to the throne, the schemes died with him.

It seems that he relied almost entirely on his own Macedonian generals and soldiers and had little trust in the Greeks, and that he was prepared to make a place for the Persian nobility. But the various projects which modern scholars enjoy attributing to Alexander are highly speculative, without serious foundation in the available evidence. Anyway, Alexander's death put an end to them all, and to his empire too. A half-century of internecine warfare among his Macedonian generals followed, out of which the Hellenistic territorial and military pattern emerged. Ptolemy, one of the generals closest to Alexander, succeeded very quickly in obtaining control of Egypt. Macedon itself and the Greek mainland fell to the successors of Antigonus – the least satisfactory portion of the inheritance, both for geographical reasons and because Greek resistance to Macedonian rule never wholly ceased, especially in the Peloponnese, where it was led by the Achaean League, and in Rhodes and other Aegean islands. The other major division was in the east, centring on Syria and Mesopotamia, where with Ptolemy's help Seleucus eventually won the throne.

Hellenistic political history is a wearying one, monotonous and often ugly, of unceasing warfare, bad faith and not infrequent assassination. The three main kingdoms struggled without end to enlarge their territories at each other's expense. A number of smaller kingdoms, the most important being Pergamum in Asia Minor, were able to achieve a more or less independent existence by playing one great power against another. Internally, too, bitter dynastic struggles were far from rare. And then there were independence movements, not only among the Greek cities and leagues but also in Judaea under the Maccabees. By the beginning of the second century B.C. they were all much weakened, and at that moment Rome moved in, having just completed the process of winning control over the western Mediterranean. The incorporation of the Hellenistic world into the Roman Empire was a long piecemeal process, completed, except for some further tidying up, when Antony and Cleopatra were defeated at Actium in 31 B.C.

Greek Cities and Absolute Monarchs

By Alexander's time the Greeks had had much experience of settlement among other, 'barbarian' people, and in some areas, such as Caria in Asia Minor or the Crimea, of much intermarriage and cultural fusion. The Hellenistic phenomenon, however, was of a different order and on a vaster scale. For half a century whole armies of Macedonians and Greeks spent their lives fighting abroad. Eventually they were settled in the conquered areas, where they together with still more migrants from Greece formed a new governing class, holding the wealth and power while the natives remained the subordinate, working population. By no means all the newcomers became men of wealth and leisure. A large middle class of soldier-settlers was also created, holding land from the king in return for military service, a status which they transmitted to their descendants.

Everywhere Alexander and his successors founded new cities modelled on the Greek (or refounded old ones). Some, like Alexandria, Antioch and Seleucia-on-the-Tigris, became great metropolises, far surpassing even classical Athens in size and prosperity. (These three reached and perhaps exceeded half a million in population, to be matched only by Rome and Carthage.) The characteristic elements of a Greek *polis* were transplanted: the Agora and temples, the gymnasia and stoas, assemblies, councils and magistrates. And of course the immigrants and their descendants spoke Greek, a modified Attic dialect which became uniform throughout most of the

Hellenistic world (best known today as the Greek of the New Testament). The educated and the old ruling elements among the conquered people quickly adopted the Greek tongue and much of Greek culture. The natives of the lower classes, however, clung tenaciously to their own speech and writing – Egyptian, for example, or Aramaic, the original language of the Gospels – and this was the most obvious external sign of the fundamental cleavage in the population.

As for the government, the official language was Greek and so were many of the legal formalities. The reality, however, was decidedly not Greek. There was nothing in the Greek experience which allowed for territorial states of the size of Pergamum, approximately 70,000 square miles at its maximum (as against some 1,000 in Attica), not to mention the Seleucid empire, which once took in perhaps a million and a half square miles. Nor could the rulers have found a way to translate Greek political and administrative practices to this new scale had they wished. Not even the tyrants were an adequate model, and anyway tyranny was always held, by all schools of thought, to be the denial of truly Hellenic political existence. The Hellenistic kings were from the very beginning absolute monarchs in the most literal sense, ruling personally and dynastically, the sole source of law, free to deal with everyone, from the lowest to the highest, by arbitrary decision, a prerogative they exercised frequently enough. Naturally there was a large bureaucracy: there was no other way to conduct the affairs of state, which became all-embracing. Yet so personal was the sovereignty that the 'country' a monarch ruled had no name. Ptolemy and Seleucus and their successors were kings, but they were not king 'of' anything, Egypt or Babylonia or Persia; not only in principle but also in the official language, whether in their internal edicts or in treaties and other international documents. Egypt was a proper geographical term, but the Ptolemaic territory was more extensive, and the Seleucids lacked even such a well-defined core in their sphere.

Historically the roots of this system lay in the monarchical régimes long established in the ancient Near East and automatically adopted by the Macedonian conquerors. This was the overriding reality (except with the Antigonids), and though cities on the Greek model were introduced as a new element, their life of necessity differed in quality from that of previous periods in Greek history. The Hellenistic city was not a political organization but an administrative centre. It performed various community services, connected with food and water supply, for example, or with religion and education; it also was responsible for tax collection, the administration of justice and other tasks assigned to it by the king. The formalities and, to a degree, the ideology went even farther: everyone was the king's subject, but in the cities, with respect to local affairs, the status of citizen was highly prized, as if the old days still survived. Whatever the honour may have signified socially and psychologically, it was rather empty politically: no city had autonomy, or even any genuine initiative, in the decisive fields of legislation and financial policy; judicial decisions were subject to the appellate jurisdiction of the king; foreign affairs were entirely in his hands. No wonder the gymnasium became the real focus of Greek city-life, not the assembly and the council-chamber, and the gymnasiarch tended to become the ranking city official. It was altogether fitting that most of the new foundations took even their names from a king or queen: Alexandria, Antioch, Seleucia, Laodicea, Berenice – these are the names which were repeated over and over again.

Only on the mainland of Greece and the Aegean islands (most notably Rhodes) was there a struggle of some consequence to maintain traditional Greek political life. Wherever the Antigonid dynasty obtained full control, the Hellenistic pattern prevailed, for the Antigonids became (or tried to become) as absolute as their rivals in the east. However, their situation was significantly different: at home, where they were based, they remained Macedonian kings ruling Macedonians and not free to assume the Near-Eastern style of absolute authority; and in their conquered Greek territory there was no underlying non-Greek population. Often their control was weak, sometimes it was actually broken in one area or another, so that until the Romans finally took over in the middle of the second century B.C., one may speak of a continuation of the *polis* in old Greece, though watered down and modified.

The institution which crowned the whole structure of Hellenistic monarchy was ruler-worship. Alexander had taken the critical first step and his successors followed his lead, although it required about two generations for the practice to become fixed and nearly universal. The divinity of the reigning monarch (often together with his consort) was a very ancient concept, most notably in Egypt. Hence where it was traditionally an element in monarchy, the natives found it natural, even necessary from their point of view, to accept the conqueror as a god and to pay him due homage. But the whole idea was alien to the Persians, for example, among the conquered people and most certainly to the Macedonians and Greeks, despite some few aberrant exceptions, and it is therefore remarkable how quickly and easily they all fell into line. This was true in old Greece, where an odd situation prevailed: the Antigonids were not worshipped in Macedon itself, while they had their shrines in many Greek cities, as did other Hellenistic rulers as well, in their case usually in return for a benefaction.

There is probably nothing in Greek history more elusive than the psychology of emperor-worship. We are told that Demosthenes sneered openly when Alexander in 324 commanded the Greeks to recognize him as the son of Zeus. No doubt there were many sceptics, in this and later generations.

The kings themselves, though they required the cult, never spoke or wrote or decreed as gods, or even as the sons of gods. Active opposition to the cult was extremely rare; when it occurred it had unmistakable political overtones and was dealt with as a political offence, a threat to the régime, not as heresy or blasphemy. Yet to reduce the institution merely to politics, to a kind of shadow-boxing in which no one believed, would be wrong (as with the Delphic oracle in another age). Millions of people participated in the ceremonies, vast sums were spent on buildings and statues and dedications, and there were innumerable, visible links with cult 'proper' – altogether too much for mere political propaganda. Our inability to grasp the sense of the institution stems from our sharp lines of demarcation. Not even Athens in the Enlightenment drew them that way. When Sophocles died he was transformed by a cult-group of Asclepius into Dexion, the Receiver, and was given a small shrine. That was cult in the strict sense, and it is useless to object that in his lifetime no Athenian thought Sophocles to be anything but a mortal, true as that statement no doubt is. In the Hellenistic world, with its very heterogeneous population and its mixed historical antecedents, the possibilities of complication, of far more overlapping between the human and the divine, the sacred and the secular, were limitless. Whatever the nuances, the fact remains that ruler-cult became an integral part of Hellenistic polytheism among all sections of the population.

Polytheistic religions are by their nature tolerant and highly adaptable: new gods are incorporated, old gods acquire new attributes, old and new elements are combined. Greek religion exemplified these possibilities throughout its history, as in the striking example of the identification of Zeus with the Egyptian sun-god Ammon, but in the Hellenistic age the process of fusion (or syncretism) reached new heights, reflecting the new mixed society. Ruler-worship was one manifestation. The Isis cult, with its trinitarianism, was another significant instance; the partial Hellenization of the Israelite religion still another. And all these 'new' religions were universal; that is to say, they were not rooted in any given city, district or country, but, if successful, spread to all parts of the Hellenistic world and eventually to the Roman west as well.

Hellenistic religion was further characterized by its other-worldliness. The Hellenistic Greek still recognized the old Olympian pantheon and still participated, at least vicariously, in the public cults of his city. He also continued to seek supernatural assistance in his everyday affairs, and it is significant that now not only the goddess Tyche (Fortune) acquired particular prominence but also astrology, an ancient Babylonian art which the Greeks had previously ignored despite their great interest in astronomy. But genuine religious life became increasingly that of the mystery religions, with their stress on purification, initiation, communion and, in one way or another, redemption. Religion was much more personal than heretofore. Because the *polis* had lost its all-embracing community quality, it could no longer be the centre of man's spiritual life. Each individual now had to find his salvation himself, between himself and the divine in a direct communion.

Developments in philosophy ran a comparable course. They, too, turned men inward, setting their backs to the material world. In so far as classical ethics were based on the community of the city-state, they became meaningless in the Hellenistic absolute monarchies. Classical philosophers believed in human inequality, and in political action resting on that premiss. Stoicism, the dominant Hellenistic philosophy, began by preaching the brotherhood of man under a single divine law, but in a negative or passive sense – wisdom and virtue required indifference to material pains and pleasures, to wealth or poverty, slavery or civic rights. Hellenistic philosophy and religion thus had a common meeting-ground, though the one was rational and coldly intellectual in its arguments, the other emotional and often orgiastic, offering rites instead of reasons. Each on its own level gave consolation and hope in a world in which the material prospects were poor and politics were no longer subject to rational analysis, in which, therefore, ethics had to be divorced from society, and even more from current politics.

Greeks and Romans

Stoic doctrine was not static, and its history is full of complexities and even contradictions. For example, it quickly took up astrology on the one hand, and on the other hand it made interesting contributions to physical theory. Above all, it was Stoic quietism which underwent important changes. Indifference to social position – and hence acceptance of whatever status one happened to have – was turned into a doctrine of vocation and duty, especially for rulers. This shift was largely the work of the Rhodian school, whose chief figures were Panaetius and the immensely learned Poseidonius (131–51 B.C.), Cicero's teacher in philosophy. Stoicism then became the main philosophical school of the Romans as well. Among the outstanding Roman Stoics were Seneca (who held high office for a long time under Nero) and the emperor Marcus Aurelius. For such men of action obviously the brotherhood of man and the rule of natural reason had altogether different overtones from those of early Stoicism. The object now was to find a moral basis on which to rule an empire, and after Augustus established monarchical government in Rome this was further narrowed to rule by an absolute monarch. The king, who was also a philosopher, became the Stoic ideal, and the Cynic as well.

Roman Stoicism is but one example of the truth of Horace's

well-known line, 'Captive Greece made captive her rude conqueror'. Long before Rome took an active interest in the eastern Mediterranean she had been under considerable cultural influence from the Greeks, through their settlements in southern Italy. It was from Cumae, for example, that the Romans learned the alphabet. For a long time, the absorption of borrowings from Greek culture seems not to have created any difficulties. By the first half of the second century B.C., however, the influences – in religion and philosophy, the drama and historiography – had become so massive that some Romans, like the elder Cato, protested long and loudly. But the Catos were not to prevail. The gradual conquest of the Hellenistic world flooded Rome and Italy with Greek ideas, Greek works of art and Greek-speaking slaves. Thereafter, in most fields of endeavour (with the notable exceptions of law, the army and political administration) it is impossible to discuss Roman ideas apart from their Greek models or inspiration. The eastern part of the Empire, indeed, was in many ways still Greek – Hellenistic Greek – to the end. There is no more important witness than early Christianity. Beginning with St Paul, the newest of the mystery religions was preached to Greeks, Hellenized Jews and other Hellenized peoples of the eastern provinces in the language, and with the techniques, of the Greek rhetoricians. The Old Testament was normally quoted not from the Hebrew text, which relatively few Christians or their prospective proselytes could read, but from the Septuagint, the Greek translation prepared in the third century B.C. Christian theology first received a systematic philosophical cast from men who were steeped in the traditions of Greek philosophy from Plato to later Stoicism. Apologists on both sides even debated, in all seriousness, the question of priority between Homer and Moses. The pagan defenders of Homer were fighting a hopeless rearguard action. A wholly new phase of western history had already begun.

CHRONOLOGICAL TABLE

800 B.C.

Olympic Games instituted
776

? Composition of *Iliad* and
Odyssey

Western 'colonization'
begins *c.* 750

700 B.C.   ? Hesiod

Tyranny of Cypselids in   Archilochus *fl.* 650
Corinth, *c.* 650–585
Black Sea 'colonization'
begins *c.* 650

Second Messenian War

Thales, ? 600
600 B.C.   Sappho and Alcaeus *fl.* 600

Archonship of Solon 594

600 B.C.

Tyranny of Peisistratids in
    Athens c. 545–10

                            Pindar born 518

Cleisthenes reforms the
    Athenian constitution 508

500 B.C.

Ionian Revolt 499–94
Persian Wars 490–79

Delian League and
    Athenian Empire
    478–404
  Ostracism of Cimon 461   Temple of Zeus at Olympia
                            completed 456
                            Aeschylus dies 456

Treasury moved to Athens   Aristophanes born c. 450
    454
  Peloponnesian War   Hippocratic school of medi-
    431–404   cine at its peak 440–390
  Plague at Athens 430–26   Pindar dies c. 438
  Death of Pericles 429   Parthenon completed 432
  Death of Cleon 422   Herodotus dies between
  Peace of Nicias 421   430 and 424
                            Plato born c. 429

  Sicilian expedition 415–13 Sophocles and Euripides
                            die 406
                          Erechtheum completed 404
                        Thucydides dies between

400 B.C.   404 and 399
  Trial of Socrates 399

                        Aristophanes dies c. 385
                        Plato founds the Academy
                          c. 385
                        Demosthenes born 384

400 B.C.

Thebes defeats Sparta at
Leuctra 371
Philip II King of Macedon
359–36

Plato dies 347

Battle of Chaeronea 338
Alexander the Great 336–23
Foundation of Alexandria
331

End of democracy in
Athens 322

Ptolemy I and Seleucus I
assume royal titles 305

Isocrates dies 338
Diogenes the Cynic dies *c.* 325

Demosthenes put to death
322
Aristotle dies 322
Menander writes the
Dyskolos 316
Zeno (founder of Stoic
school) comes to Athens
313
Epicurus opens school in
Athens 306

300 B.C.

Elements of Euclid *c.* 300

Theophrastus dies between
288 and 285

Callimachus dies *c.* 240

Archimedes killed 212

200 B.C.

Rome defeats Philip V of
Macedon at
Cynoscephalae 197

Great Altar of Pergamum
c. 180
Hipparchus *fl.*

Rome destroys Corinth 146

Poseidonius of Rhodes born
131
Polybius dies *c.* 118

100 B.C.

0 ——————————————————————————————————

Plutarch born *c.* 46
Hero of Alexandria *fl.*

A.D. 100

Lucian born *c.* 120
Claudius Ptolemy *fl.* 120–50

Galen dies 199

A.D. 200

NOTES ON THE PLATES

1. *a*. Clay tablet from Cnossus (no. Am 826), about 1400, in Linear B script. The lower line reads *te-ko-to-ne* followed by the sign for 'man' and the numeral '5', translated 'five carpenters'.

Reproduced by courtesy of the Museum of Classical Archaeology, University of Cambridge.

b. Athens, Epigraphical Museum, no. 6739. Fragment of Pentelic marble found in the wall of a modern house in 1932, the base of a memorial to those who fell at Marathon in 490, containing two two-line metrical epigrams. The monument was presumably destroyed by the Persians in 480.

Reproduced by courtesy of Professor Gunther Klaffenbach.

c. The opening lines of Bodmer Papyrus no. 4, purchased in Egypt and now in Geneva, published by V. Martin in 1958. There are eleven sheets altogether, numbered and written on both sides, part of a codex of the plays of Menander copied in the first half of the third century A.D. These eleven sheets contain the *Dyskolos* or *Misanthrope,* first produced in Athens in 316 B.C.

Reproduced by courtesy of Professor Victor Martin.

2. The theatre at Segesta in western Sicily. Segesta was a native settlement, inland among the mountains, and was Hellenized only slowly. The theatre, usually dated about 100 B.C., reveals a style transitional from Hellenistic Greek to Roman.

3. The theatre and temple of Apollo at Delphi. The theatre is of local limestone and could seat about 5,000. The first one was built on the site, facing the valley and dominating the entire precinct, at least by the early years of the third century. Its present state is that of the rebuilding about 160, with some later modifications in details.

The Doric temple is of limestone from the Peloponnese and was built over a period of thirty years following the destruction in 373, by earthquake or landslide (or both), of an earlier temple. It was finally abandoned in the third century A.D. The external dimensions are approximately 200 by 78 feet.

Reproduced by courtesy of J. Allan Cash.

4. *a.* Châtillon-sur-Seine, Museum. The great bronze urn, 5 feet 4½ inches tall, was found in a Celtic grave excavated in 1953 at nearby Vix, along with the skeleton of a female aged thirty to thirty-five, remains of a chariot and a rich treasure in gold. The urn is the most imposing metal container that has survived from antiquity. Similar but very much smaller vessels have been found over a wide area reaching to southern Russia. The work is Greek of the sixth century. A full account of the find, beautifully illustrated, appears in the *Monuments et mémoires* of the Fondation Eugène Piot, Vol. 48 (1959).

b. British Museum, no. 1957.8–9.1. A Graeco-Scythian gold bracelet, slightly more than 3 inches wide, dated about 300.

Reproduced by courtesy of the British Museum.

c. Gela, Museo Archeologico. Such polychrome terra-cotta ante-fixes were used to cover the ends of tiles on the eaves and cornices of temples. This one, a head of Silenus, was of local manufacture, probably in the period 470–460.

5. *Kouroi* is the modern term, from the Greek word meaning 'youth', for the archaic statues of male nudes, in stone or bronze, of which more than 200 are now known, ranging in date from about 650 to about 460. More accurately, the statues of the final twenty-five years have already achieved a classical style and are grouped in an 'Epilogue' in Miss G. M. A. Richter's book, *Kouroi* (2nd ed., Phaidon, 1960).

a. Athens, National Museum, no. 3851 (no. 136 in Miss Richter's catalogue). Six-foot statue of Croesus, of Parian marble, found in 1936 at Anavysos in southern Attica and dated between about 540 and 520. Traces of red paint are still visible on the hair, headband, pupils and pubic hair. Inscribed on the base, found in 1938, is a metrical distich which reads, in the translation by P. Friedländer and H. B. Hoffleit, *Epigrammata* (Univ. of California, 1948), p. 86: 'Stand and weep by the tomb of Croesus dead, whom rushing Ares destroyed one day as he fought in the forefront.' The name Croesus, originally Lydian, had come into use among the Greeks, at least in the east.

Reproduced from *Kouroi* by Gisela M. A. Richter (Phaidon Press Ltd, 1960) by permission of the publishers.

b. Athens, Acropolis Museum, no. 698 (no. 190 in Miss Richter's catalogue, the first in her 'Epilogue'). Parian marble, 2 feet 10 inches high, found on the Acropolis (the body in 1865, the head in 1888), probably a dedication not long before the Persians invaded and destroyed the city in 480 (and incidentally smashed this statue). 'Then, quite suddenly,' Sir Kenneth Clark writes of this statue in *The Nude* (Penguin ed., p. 27), 'there appears before us the perfect human body . . . the first [surviving] beautiful nude in art'.

Reproduced by courtesy of the Acropolis Museum, Athens.

6. Delphi, Museum, no. 3484. Bronze statue of a charioteer, 5 feet 11 inches, found in three pieces in 1896. The original monument, which stood near the temple of Apollo, included the chariot drawn by four horses, but only small fragments of these have survived. Parts of the inscribed base have also been recovered, revealing that the monument was dedicated to Apollo by Polyzalus, tyrant of Gela in Sicily, to commemorate a victory in the Pythian Games, probably in 474.

Reproduced by courtesy of The Mansell Collection and Alinari.

7. Athens, National Museum, no. 15,118. Full-length bronze, 4 feet 3 inches, dated on stylistic grounds shortly after the middle of the fourth century. The subject cannot be fixed with any certainty. The statue was found in 1925 in the Bay of Marathon, perhaps from a shipwrecked consignment of works of art on the way to Italy.

Reproduced by courtesy of Alison Frantz.

8. Silver coins (all actual size), Fitzwilliam Museum, Cambridge. The most common size was the tetradrachm, followed by the drachma and didrachm. Larger coins were extremely rare before the Hellenistic period and were jubilee medallions rather than proper coins.

Reproduced by courtesy of the Fitzwilliam Museum, Cambridge.

a. Athens, tetradrachm. These 'owls' with the head of Athena in a crested Athenian helmet remained relatively unchanged in design from the late sixth century on, and were the most famous and widely used of all Greek coins. The three-leaved olive spray was introduced in 490 or soon after and is believed to commemorate the victory at Marathon.

b. Syracuse, decadrachm, first minted in 413 to celebrate the victory over the Athenian expeditionary force. Obverse: a four-horse chariot at the gallop, Nike crowning the charioteer. Reverse: Arethusa and dolphins. Signed by Euaenetus (artist's signatures being most uncommon on coins).

c. Chalcidian League, tetradrachm on the lighter 'Phoenician' standard. The League was established in 392 with Olynthus as its centre. This particular coin is an early one in the series, which lasted until perhaps 358. Obverse: head of Apollo. Reverse: the word 'Chalcidians' around a seven-stringed lyre.

d. Tetradrachm of Alexander minted at Amphipolis, probably soon after his death in 323. Obverse: Heracles in a lion's skin. Reverse: Zeus enthroned with sceptre and eagle, the name 'Alexander'.

9. The Parthenon, the temple of Athena on the Athenian Acropolis, was built in the third quarter of the fifth century and remained relatively intact through a long variegated history until it was bombarded by a Venetian force in 1687, the Turks having converted it into an arsenal. In 1799 Lord Elgin, then British ambassador to Turkey, removed a great deal of the sculpture to England, and the 'Elgin marbles' were purchased for the British Museum in 1816. The collection includes figures from the two triangular pediments, which were badly shattered (especially the principal figures). The pediments were more than 90 feet long, about 3 feet deep and 11 feet high at the centre, so that the largest sculptures were nearly twice life size.

Reproduced by courtesy of the British Museum.

a. The east pediment, above the entrance, had as its theme the birth of Athena. These two figures, which were near the right angle, represent two nymphs or goddesses, but it is impossible to identify them.

b. The theme of the west pediment was the contest in wonderworking by which Athena and Poseidon competed for Attica. This figure, from the left corner, represents the personification of a river, probably the Ilissus, who had been lying at ease and had then raised himself on his left arm and swung round to watch the contest.

10. The Erechtheum on the Acropolis in Athens, a temple dedicated jointly to Athena and Poseidon-Erechtheus, located on the site of the legendary contest between the two gods (see the previous

note), and completed in 404. The unusual plan of the building can be explained in part, but not wholly, by the very irregular ground-level and by the desire to unite a number of ancient sanctuaries that had existed on the spot.

Reproduced by courtesy of J. Allan Cash.

11. A detail from the Erechtheum, showing its unusually elaborate ornamentation and the perfection of the workmanship, some of which, as has been stated in the text, was carried out by slave labour.

Reproduced by courtesy of Alison Frantz.

12. Athens, National Museum, no. 870. A marble tombstone from Athens, more than 6 feet high and 3 feet wide, dated about 330. It was carved from a single block. The original frame, made separately, is lost.

Reproduced by courtesy of Mrs S. A. Adam.

13. One of the metopes (as the sculpted portions of the frieze of a Doric temple are called), a running centaur, from the ruins of the large sixth-century temple of Hera discovered in 1934 at Foce del Sele near Paestum on the Gulf of Salerno in southern Italy. The considerable remains of the frieze, now displayed in the Museum at Paestum, depict scenes from the Heracles legends.

Reproduced from *Heraion alla Foce del Sele*, by Dr U. Zanotti-Bianco and Signora P. Zancani Montuoro by courtesy of the authors and of the Istituto Poligrafico dello Stato, Rome.

14–15. The three architectural orders, exemplified by three Athen-ian temples. The Doric order was created in the Peloponnese in the seventh century, the Ionic east of the Aegean in the following century, while the Corinthian, an offshoot of Ionic and not an independent order, was an invention of the late fifth century which did not be-come common in temple exteriors until Roman times. The most obvious differences are in the columns and their capitals and in the treatment of the frieze. Detailed descriptions can be found in the architectural works mentioned in the bibliography.

Doric – the Parthenon (see note to no. 9).

Reproduced by courtesy of J. Allan Cash.

Ionic – the small temple, without side colonnades, of Nike (Victory) on the Acropolis, standing immediately on the right as one ascends the steps to the citadel. Its erection was authorized by the Assembly in 449, and it may not have been completed until a quarter-century had elapsed.

Reproduced by courtesy of the Radio Times Hulton Picture Library.

Corinthian – some of the sixteen columns which survive of the temple of Olympian Zeus, completed by the emperor Hadrian probably in A.D. 132, but begun 300 years earlier.

Reproduced by courtesy of J. Allan Cash.

16. Olympia, Museum. Sculptures from the temple of Zeus, a Doric structure about the same size as the Parthenon, completed in 456. The theme on the west pediment was a battle between Centaurs and Lapiths, the latter being given the victory by Apollo. The god occupied the central position on the pediment, nearly 11 feet in height.

Reproduced by courtesy of J. Allan Cash.

17. Rome, Museo delle Terme, no. 152. A three-sided relief in Parian marble, of undetermined purpose, incorrectly known as the 'Ludovisi throne' from the place where it was found in Rome in 1887. Even the scenes cannot be explained with any certainty, but the central panel, 4 feet 8 inches wide and 3 feet 6 inches high, probably represents the birth of Aphrodite from the sea. The workmanship is south Italian or Sicilian, of about 460, and it introduced the female nude into Greek sculpture, so to speak.

Reproduced from a cast by courtesy of the Museum of Classical Archaeology, University of Cambridge.

18. British Museum, no. D161. A polychrome terra-cotta, $5\frac{1}{2}$ inches high, found in Capua, probably of the third century.

Reproduced by courtesy of the Radio Times Hulton Picture Library.

19. Athens, National Museum, no. 804. A so-called Dipylon amphora from the Kerameikos, the great cemetery outside the western gates of Athens. Seven more or less complete Dipylon vases are extant, this one being the earliest, probably from the middle of the eighth century or a little before. Five feet tall, the vase served as a funeral monument into which libations for the dead were poured, running through a hole at the bottom into the grave itself. A recent detailed analysis will be found in Jean M. Davison, *Attic Geometric Workshops* (published as Vol. 16 of *Yale Classical Studies*, 1961).

Reproduced by courtesy of the National Museum, Athens.

20. British Museum, no. B210. An amphora, 16¼ inches high, signed by Exekias, one of the great masters of Athenian black-figured pottery, who worked between about 550 and 520. This jug, found in an Etruscan tomb in Vulci, shows the god Dionysus holding vine-branches and receiving a drinking-cup from a boy named Oinopion; on the other side, Achilles slaying Penthesilea.

Reproduced by courtesy of the British Museum.

21. British Museum, no. 47.9–9.7. A red-figured Athenian amphora, 2 feet high, manufactured about 440, found in an Etruscan tomb in Vulci. The muse Terpsichore is seated in the middle playing a triangular harp; in front of her the legendary singer Musaeus holds a lyre and staff, at the left Melusa holds a pair of flutes.

Reproduced by courtesy of the British Museum.

22. British Museum, no. 1928.7–19.1. A cup, 3¾ inches high, from Corinth, of the late seventh century. The shape, probably invented in Corinth, has a continuous history there from early in the archaic period. This exceptionally well-preserved example is one of the earliest and finest in the fully developed style. See the classic study by H. Payne, *Necrocorinthia* (O.U.P., 1931).

Reproduced by courtesy of the British Museum.

23. British Museum, no. 268. A bronze head, 1 foot high, found in 1861 in the ruins of the temple of Apollo in Cyrene. Probably to be dated in the middle of the fourth century, the head is one of the earliest individualized sculptures, clearly of a native North African.

Reproduced by courtesy of the British Museum.

24. Reconstruction of the west front of the great altar erected in Pergamum about 180, dedicated to Zeus and Athena and placed on a large rectangular terrace overlooking the Agora. The outside stair-case measured 66 feet in width. The 'great frieze', 7 feet 6 inches high, almost 400 feet long, contained more than 100 slabs depicting the war between the gods and the giants. The ruins of the altar were excavated in the last decades of the nineteenth century, and the remains were brought to the national museum in (East) Berlin, where the front of the building was reconstructed.

Reproduced from Vol. III, 1 (Plates) of the Pergamum publications of the (Ehemals) Staatliche Museen, Berlin.

BIBLIOGRAPHY

(*Note*: Penguin books are published in Harmondsworth, Middlesex; all others in London or at a university unless otherwise indicated.)

ORIGINAL SOURCES IN TRANSLATION

The most complete collection, containing both the Greek original and English translation, is in the Loeb Classical Library (Heinemann). A considerable number of translations have also been issued by Penguin. New titles continue to appear in both collections and also as separate publications. Of the latter, attention should be directed to the verse translations by Richmond Lattimore of the *Iliad*, Hesiod and Pindar; and to the translations of all surviving Greek tragedies published under the editorship of Lattimore and David Grene (9 vols., Chicago, 1953–9).

The following are useful anthologies in English of sources on special subjects:

Finley, M. I., ed., *The Greek Historians* (Chatto & Windus, 1959)

Cohen, M. R., and Drabkin, I. E., eds., *Source Book in Greek Science* (Harvard, 1958)

Warmington, E. H., ed., *Greek Geography* (Dent, 1934)

Barker, Sir Ernest, *From Alexander to Constantine* (O.U.P., 1956) Texts illustrating the history of Greek social and political ideas in the Hellenistic and Roman periods.

Grant, F. C., ed., *Hellenistic Religions* (N.Y.: Liberal Arts Press, 1953)

GENERAL

The Oxford Classical Dictionary (O.U.P., 1949). The best one-volume encyclopedia.

Everyman's Classical Atlas (Dent, 1961)

The Cambridge Ancient History (C.U.P., 1923–39). Volumes V–VIII deal with classical and Hellenistic Greek history.

Grote, George, *A History of Greece*, originally published 1846–56 in twelve volumes and several times reprinted; still rewarding reading.

Bury, J. B., *A History of Greece to the Death of Alexander the Great* (3rd ed., Macmillan, 1951). Since 1909 the standard English one-volume history, emphasizing political and military events.

Hammond, N. G. L., *A History of Greece to 322 B.C.* (O.U.P., 1959). A recent work with much the same emphases.

Cook, R. M., *The Greeks Till Alexander* (Thames & Hudson, 1961). In the series, *Ancient Peoples and Places*, with stress in text and pictures on material culture.

Dickinson, G. Lowes, *The Greek View of Life* (repr., Methuen, 1961)

Kitto, H. D. F., *The Greeks* (rev. ed., Penguin, 1957). A long impressionistic essay rather than a formal history.

Ehrenberg, V., *The Greek State* (Oxford: Blackwell, 1960)

Glotz, G., *The Greek City and Its Institutions* (Routledge & Kegan Paul, 1929)

SPECIAL TOPICS AND PERIODS

Special Topics

Cary, M., *The Geographic Background of Greek and Roman History* (O.U.P., 1949)

Glotz, G., *Ancient Greece at Work* (Routledge & Kegan Paul, 1926)

Michell, H., *The Economics of Ancient Greece* (rev. ed., Cambridge: Heffer, 1957)

Finley, M. I., ed., *Slavery in Classical Antiquity* (Cambridge: Heffer, 1960). Eleven articles and a bibliographical essay.

Hasebroek, J., *Trade and Politics in Ancient Greece* (Bell, 1933)

Adcock, Sir F. E., *The Greek and Macedonian Art of War* (Univ. of California, 1957)

Gardiner, E. N., *Athletics of the Ancient World* (O.U.P., 1955)

Licht, H., *Sexual Life in Ancient Greece* (Routledge & Kegan Paul, 1932)

Michell, H., *Sparta* (C.U.P., 1952)

Cook, J. M., *The Greeks in Ionia and the East* (Thames & Hudson, 1962). In the *Ancient Peoples and Places* series.

Burn, A. R., *Persia and the Greeks* (Edward Arnold, 1962)

Woodhead, A. G., *The Greeks in the West* (Thames & Hudson, 1962). In the *Ancient Peoples and Places* series.

Homeric and Archaic

Starr, C. G., *The Origins of Greek Civilization, 1100–650 B.C.* (Cape, 1962)

Page, D. L., *History and the Homeric Iliad* (Univ. of California, 1959)

Finley, M. I., *The World of Odysseus* (Chatto & Windus, 1956; Penguin, 1962)

Andrewes, A., *The Greek Tyrants* (Hutchinson, 1956)

Boardman, J., *The Greeks Overseas* (Penguin, 1964)

Dunbabin, T. J., *The Western Greeks* (O.U.P., 1948)

Classical Athens

Ehrenberg, V., *The People of Aristophanes. A Sociology of Old Attic Comedy* (2nd ed., Oxford: Blackwell, 1951)

Jones, A. H. M., *Athenian Democracy* (Oxford: Blackwell, 1957)

Zimmern, A. E., *The Greek Commonwealth. Politics and Economics in Fifth-Century Athens* (4th ed., O.U.P., 1924)

Hellenistic

Tarn, W. W., *Alexander the Great* (C.U.P., 1948). Vol. I, The Narrative; Vol. II, Sources and Studies.

Burn, A. R., *Alexander the Great and the Hellenistic Empire* (English Univ. Press, 1947)

Rostovtzeff, M., *The Social & Economic History of the Hellenistic World* (3 vols., O.U.P., 1953)

Tarn, W. W., and Griffith, G. T., *Hellenistic Civilisation* (3rd ed., Arnold, 1952)

LITERATURE

Marrou, H. I., *A History of Education in Antiquity* (Sheed & Ward, 1956)

Kenyon, F. G., *Books and Readers in Ancient Greece and Rome* (2nd ed., O.U.P., 1951)

Kirk, G. S., *The Songs of Homer* (C.U.P., 1962)

Bowra, C. M., *Greek Lyric Poetry from Alcman to Simonides* (2nd ed., O.U.P., 1961)

Jones, John, *On Aristotle and Greek Tragedy* (Chatto & Windus, 1962)

Lucas, D. W., *The Greek Tragic Poets* (2nd ed., Cohen & West, 1959)

Bieber, M., *The History of the Greek and Roman Theater* (2nd ed., Princeton, 1961). Very fully illustrated.

Webster, T. B. L., *Greek Theatre Production* (Methuen, 1956)

Bury, J. B., *The Ancient Greek Historians* (repr., N.Y.: Dover, 1958)

Kennedy, G., *The Art of Persuasion in Greece* (Princeton, 1963)

Körte, A., *Hellenistic Poetry* (Columbia, 1929)

RELIGION, PHILOSOPHY AND SCIENCE

Rose, H. J., *A Handbook of Greek Mythology* (6th ed., Methuen, 1958)

Guthrie, W. K. C., *The Greeks and Their Gods* (Methuen, 1954)

Murray, Gilbert, *Five Stages of Greek Religion* (repr., Watts, 1946)

Snell, B., *The Discovery of the Mind. The Greek Origins of European Thought* (Oxford: Blackwell, 1953)

Dodds, E. R., *The Greeks and the Irrational* (Univ. of California, 1951)

Adkins, A. W. H., *Merit and Responsibility. A Study in Greek Values* (O.U.P., 1960)

Armstrong, A. H., *An Introduction to Ancient Philosophy* (3rd ed., Methuen, 1957)

Guthrie, W. K. C., *A History of Greek Philosophy* (C.U.P., Vol. I 1962, Vol. II 1965)

Cornford, F. M., *Before and After Socrates* (C.U.P., 1950)

Drachmann, A. B., *Atheism in Pagan Antiquity* (Copenhagen: Gyldendal, 1922)

Kirk, G. S., and Raven, J. E., *The Presocratic Philosophers. A Critical History with a Selection of Texts* (corr. repr., C.U.P., 1962)

Friedländer, P., *Plato*. (Routledge & Kegan Paul, Vol. I 1958, Vol. II 1964)

Grube, G. M. A., *Plato's Thought* (Methuen, 1935)

Allan, D. J., *The Philosophy of Aristotle* (Home Univ. Library, 1952)

BIBLIOGRAPHY

Randall, J. H., Jr, *Aristotle* (Columbia, 1960)

Bevan, E. R., *Stoics and Sceptics* (repr., Cambridge: Heffer, 1959)

Baldry, H. C., *The Unity of Mankind in Greek Thought* (C.U.P. 1965)

Nock, A. D., *Conversion. The Old and the New in Religion from Alexander the Great to Augustine of Hippo* (O.U.P., 1933)

Jaeger, W., *Early Christianity and Greek Paideia* (O.U.P., 1962)

Farrington, B., *Greek Science* (rev. ed., Penguin, 1961)

Sambur'sky, S., *The Physical World of the Greeks* (Routledge & Kegan Paul, 1956)

THE VISUAL ARTS

Wycherley, R. E., *How the Greeks Built Cities* (2nd ed., Macmillan, 1962)

Carpenter, Rhys, *The Esthetic Basis of Greek Art* (repr., Indiana Univ., 1959)

Lawrence, A. W., *Greek Architecture* (Penguin, 1957)

Plommer, Hugh, *Ancient and Classical Architecture* (Longmans Green, 1956)

Carpenter, Rhys, *Greek Sculpture* (Chicago, 1960)

Lullies, R., and Hirmer, M., *Greek Sculpture* (2nd ed., Thames & Hudson, 1960)

Bluemel, C., *Greek Sculptors at Work* (Phaidon, 1955)

Corbett, P. E., *The Sculpture of the Parthenon* (Penguin, 1959)

Charbonneaux, J., *Greek Bronzes* (Elek Books, 1962)

Clark, Kenneth, *The Nude* (Murray, 1956; Penguin, 1960)

Robertson, Martin, *Greek Painting* (Skira, 1959)

Cook, R. M., *Greek Painted Pottery* (Methuen, 1960)

Beazley, J. D., *The Development of Attic Black-Figure* (Univ. of California, 1951)

Seltman, C., *Greek Coins* (2nd ed., Methuen, 1955)

INDEX

MORE ABOUT PENGUINS
AND PELICANS

If you have enjoyed reading this book you may wish to know that *Penguin Book News* appears every month. It is an attractively illustrated magazine containing a complete list of books published by Penguins and still in print, together with details of the month's new books. A specimen copy will be sent free on request.

Penguin Book News is obtainable from most bookshops; but you may prefer to become a regular subscriber at 3s for twelve issues. Just write to Dept. EP, Penguin Books Ltd, Harmondsworth, Middlesex, enclosing a cheque or postal order, and you will be put on the mailing list.

Another Pelican by M. I. Finley is described on the following page.

Note: *Penguin Book News* is not
available in the U.S.A.